MW01225746

Healing
FROM THE HEART AND MIND

Ron Wilding

Copyright Ron Wilding 2001

All correspondence to

Ron Wilding, 18A Parari Street,

Warana, Queensland 4575

Telephone: 07 5493 2926

This book is copyright. Apart from any fair dealing for the purpose of private
study, research, criticism or review, as permitted under the copyright Act,
no part may be reproduced by any process without
written permission from the publisher.

All rights reserved.

ISBN 0 - 9578071 - 9 - 8

Typeset and printed by

The Australian Printing Factory

P.O. Box 5366, Maroochydore B.C.,

Queensland, Australia 4558

Telephone: 07 5493 1088   Facsimile: 07 5493 4742

Email: print.factory@bigpond.com

First Printed in August 2001

Second Impression January 2003

Dedicated to my wife, Gloria.

Introduction

My name is Ron Wilding and I feel privileged to share my experiences with you.

The stories that are revealed within the pages of this book have been told in the hope that you can awaken your own psychic talents and feel the healing energies that are your birthright. Give thanks for this gift and use your energies wisely and for the benefit of all.

A smile and a kind encouraging word can enrich and heal the lives of others. Such simple deeds will lead you to the power of Spirit that lives within.

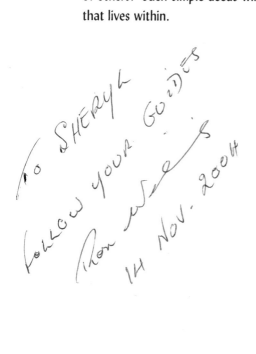

To Sheryl
Follow your Guides
Ron Wilding
14 Nov. 2004

Contents

CHAPTER ONE
The Gift of Healing

Although I have been helping people as a Psychic Healer for more than 50 years, it was not a gift that I was aware of until the age of about 19. During my childhood and adolescence I didn't have any unusual experiences that would have led me to believe that I had psychic abilities. I didn't see any apparitions, nor did I have premonitions or flashes of insight. I didn't feel different or abnormal in any way. As was quite common for a child or even an adult of that time, I had no knowledge of anything related to the psychic world. However, even if I had experienced anything unusual, I very much doubt that I would have known what to do about it anyway. In those days there really wasn't anybody to ask about such things. I was born in Fremantle, Western Australia in 1929 and spent my childhood and teenage years there. My father was the manager of a Mills and Ware biscuit factory, a company that was later taken over by Arnott's. I completed two years of high school under the noted Headmaster of the time, Jerry Dolan, and left two weeks before my fourteenth birthday. That was the average age of school leavers in those days. My first job was as an assistant in a chemist shop and as jobs go, it wasn't too bad. A while later I started working for my grandparents in their market garden business. I worked with a lot of Yugoslav immigrants there and learnt to speak the language. This was a skill that was to prove quite useful later on. I would consider that my main occupation throughout my working life was as a chef - I spent about 35 years in that industry. However, I didn't begin my training in this field until several years after I left school – I had a few more jobs in between.

My experiences with healing actually began with me studying mainstream first aid. I'm not really sure what compelled me to take the course; I just felt that it would be a useful skill to have. Besides I liked the idea of being able to help people. By 1948 I had passed 2 levels and found it to be very rewarding. Looking back, I had been drawn to the way of healing, although at that stage I had no idea of psychic healing. I certainly had no inkling of the amazing events that lay ahead for me. To compliment my progressing training, I purchased a copy of an Anatomy and Physiology textbook and studied as much as I could, eager to learn more about the human body and its functions.

In 1948 I was working as a groundsman at Perth Airport and being eager to travel, when I was offered a transfer, I jumped at the chance. The transfer took me to Port Hedland in Northern Western Australia. The first thing that hit me when I arrived there was the higher temperature, although I knew I would soon adapt. I was enthusiastic about the position and started work the following day. In 1948 Port Hedland had a population of only 120 people in town, although there was a large Aboriginal population of about 1200 in the surrounding area. My accommodation was at the Esplanade Hotel, which was 12 miles away from the airport and that meant three trips a day to work. My studies of Anatomy and Physiology were progressing and came in handy for work and sports. Minor cuts, bruises and the like were all attended to by me and all seemed to heal very quickly. However, at this point, I assumed it was due to my conventional first aid training because I was simply not aware of the gift I possessed. About 2 months after I arrived, I was invited to travel on the Flying Doctor plane to a station called Warawagine. This station was 90 miles East of Marble Bar and apparently one of the station hands had died while having a shower. The doctor who conducted an on the spot autopsy was Dr. Eric Saint. I watched him while he did the autopsy and it was determined that the man died of a heart attack. Whilst flying back to Hedland the doctor asked me if watching the autopsy had affected me in any way. My reply was that on seeing the man's heart in the condition it was, I concluded that he had died very quickly and without pain. This was not to be my only meeting with Dr. Saint. A little later I was at the hospital to sit my First Aid Certificate. I breezed through most of the questions until Dr. Saint asked me to explain to him how to determine when a person is dead. I explained to him that it was a doctor's position to tell if a person was dead and not mine. As a first aid officer, that was one of the things that I had been taught – only a doctor could pronounce a patient to be dead. Dr. Saint was not satisfied with the answer and told me to come back when I could answer the question. I did not go back to sit the exam again due to his attitude and never received any further formal qualifications in first aid. However this certainly did not hold me back in the field of healing. During my time at Port Hedland, I was very privileged to be able to speak to some of the Aboriginal elders and to learn from them some of their ways of healing. At this stage, I didn't consider myself to be a healer, but I was very interested in what they could teach me. One particular subject, 'thought transference' was a subject I was to learn more about as time went on, but this was my initial introduction to this concept.

The Aboriginal people could sit quietly for a period of time, then they would begin to mutter - to themselves I thought - but apparently it was actually to another tribal member miles away. I had to study this method for a long time before I felt that I could send a message. The knowledge that I gained from the Aboriginal people in Port Hedland was to serve me well in the future when I had an awareness of my own gift. At a study group several years later, when I had learned more about psychic healing, I was able to show how a covered object in the center of a circle, covered with a cloth, could be identified without uncovering it. I had the members of the group sit in a circle and they were then instructed to meditate and relax completely. They were then instructed to concentrate on the covered object until they felt they could recognize it. When all the members were satisfied what the object was, they were given paper and a pencil and asked to illustrate what they saw. Most of the members drew a lot of criss-crossed lines and when the object was uncovered, it was a crystal bowl. This bowl had the crossed markings of the usual crystal pattern. This concentration of thoughts on a single object showed that a person could in fact bring up any image. It was a truly amazing discovery for me and something that I would continue to learn about as time went by. After two years at Port Hedland, it was time for me to return to Perth. I resigned from the groundsman job and began as an orderly at the Royal Perth Hospital. One of my duties was to drive the Infectious Disease Ambulance. I delivered all kinds of infectious disease patients to the Shenton Park Annex of the hospital that was the specialised area for these illnesses. One day I was asked to take the ambulance to the front of the hospital to pick up a doctor and take him to a house in a particular suburb and then to the annex. The doctor sat in the front with me and when I asked him who the patient was, he explained that it was himself and that he had a severe case of German Measles. On arrival back at the hospital, I had to undergo a series of tests to see if I was immune to any diseases carried by the patients whom I had delivered to the annex. The results were positive in all of the 26 cases and the medical staff then informed me that I must have been a carrier as I had never had any of the diseases. All through my infancy, childhood and adolescence, I had not suffered any of these dreaded sicknesses that were capable of causing death or severe illness. Now many years later, I transported infected people with these diseases in the ambulance and yet never became sick myself, which was really quite amazing. In those days, there were no vaccines for most infectious diseases that people were hospitalised for. I never wore a mask, gloves or any other kind of protective clothing and the only kind of precaution taken was to spray the back of the ambulance with Formalin. It was for this reason, that driving the Infectious Disease Ambulance was not a very popular job. I can say, however, that it honestly never concerned me to do so. To this day, I have had only two mosquito borne diseases – Malaria and Ross River Fever. The Malaria attack lasted only two days the first time and I had another attack 12 years later which lasted the same time and have had no symptoms since. The Ross River attack occurred in the early 1980's and I was quite sick for three days, but was able to recover quickly, unlike many others who can take months or years to recover. My first aid training and an interest in football led me to joining the Palmyra Rugby Club as their trainer (first aid). In this role, I had to deal with a lot of every day type of accidents to the players. It was whilst I was with this club, that I began to have some rather extraordinary experiences when dealing with injuries. For me this was definitely the beginning of my career as a psychic healer, although it took me some time to realise it. On one particular day, the team was engaged in a particularly tough game when I saw a player on the ground in a maul for the ball and noticed an opposition player stamp heavily on the player's shoulder. When the referee stopped the play, I went onto the field and attended to the injured player. He had deep sprig marks on his shoulder which were already starting to bruise. I immediately began to rub the area with oil and after gently massaging for the two minutes I was allowed, he stated that the pain had eased. At half time I examined the shoulder again and found that the sprig marks had almost disappeared. The bruising was gone and the player suffered no discomfort. Another quick rub and the player finished the game with no soreness at all. Although this was a remarkable thing, I had absolutely no knowledge of psychic healing and did not consider for a moment that it had been my actions alone that had brought about such rapid healing on a fairly substantial injury.

Some time later in 1949, I went to Kalgoorlie to see a man named Christopher Martinovich. Mr Martinovich had a worldwide reputation of being able to heal all types of ailments with his healing massage and was known to have treated some Harley St (England) specialists. Harley Street in London is recognised as housing the very best medical specialists in the UK and so it appeared that Mr Martinovich certainly possessed a special talent for healing. I had heard of his amazing success and decided to meet with him. It was necessary for me to travel to Kalgoorlie because he refused to go outside the

---

town. I was prepared to make this trip because I was very interested in what he might be able to teach me. It was also an advantage in that I could speak some Yugoslavian, which was his native tongue. I was able to get some time with Mr. Martinovich and described the events of the rugby game and some other healings that I had carried out. He listened attentively, then looked me in the eye and stated that, in his opinion, he felt I was a psychic healer. I explained to him that I did not know what a psychic healer was or what that type of healing entailed. This suggestion from Mr Martinovich really didn't affect me too greatly at the time, nor did I suddenly see it as either a great gift or a huge burden to carry, but was determined to keep helping people as I had always done. However, his comments did stay with me and it would take me quite some time to really understand what my role as a healer was. Allow me to explain also that this type of healing was heavily frowned upon by the Government of the time. Anyone admitting to practising this type of healing was subsequently placed in a mental institution until their mind 'cleared' to the satisfaction of a psychiatrist, thus Mr. Martinovich advised me to admit only to massaging patients to relieve tension in muscles. Although I was interested in learning more, I could not find any courses where I could study massage at that time therefore, I relied a lot on instinct when I practiced with massage in my role as trainer/first aid attendant. Back at Perth Hospital, I was kept busy with the Infectious Disease Ambulance, and as an orderly, I carried out many different duties, one of these being a mortuary orderly. On one particular day, a plane had crashed in the hills near York, a country town 60 odd miles from Perth. Early the following morning, the bodies of the passengers began to arrive at the mortuary. Our duties, as orderlies, were to arrange the bodies on stretchers in a special cool room to await the identification process. This was my first experience at handling so many bodies in one day. It was also very disturbing because the bodies were in such bad condition due to the impact of the plane crash. I was also still very young and not used to seeing death on such a large scale. During one particular break between the Ambulances arriving, I was visibly shaken but when I sat down to rest, I remembered some advice given to me by Mr. Martinovich. He had told me that should you get upset over a situation, to sit quietly for a moment, then take a deep breath. Breathe in as much air as slowly as you can, hold it for a few seconds and then let the air out slowly. Do this three times and your nerves will return to normal and you will then be able to carry on with your duties. This worked wonders for me and I finished my day's work feeling fine, despite the rather harrowing duties that I had carried out. This advice is something that I have continued to use throughout my life, even in the most stressful situations. Deep breaths can bring about calmness very quickly. It is true that simple remedies are often the best and most effective treatment. I always enjoyed travelling and at each different location, I seemed to learn something. At this stage of my life I was moving around quite a lot and relishing the different experiences that I was encountering. My next move took me to Merredin, which was about 200 miles from Perth. Before long I was invited to join a local football team, once again in the role of trainer/first aid attendant. During one particular game, one of our youngest players hurt his back and asked me to assist him. His lower back displayed a swelling and was very hot. I assumed that a disc had been moved so I started to gently massage this area. As the pain subsided (in less than two minutes), I gently added light pressure with the flat of my hand. I heard a slight click and assumed (rightly) that the disc had gone back into place. After another few minutes massaging, the player reported that the pain had gone completely and went back onto the field to continue his game. While I had been attending to the player, I had noticed a well-dressed gentleman nearby taking note of what I was doing and he eventually came over and introduced himself to me. It turned out that he was a noted psychiatrist. He asked me a series of questions about the injury that I had just treated and he was particularly interested in finding out what I believed the injury to be, why I had come to that conclusion and also why I had treated it in the manner that I had. I did my best to explain that this was the first time that I had been called upon to treat a back pain and as there was a swelling and heat in the same area, I felt my hand being guided to the area and began to massage. He accepted my explanation and proceeded to give me some very valuable information about medical matters and we spoke for almost an hour. He then told me that although I had rightly assumed that the disc was out, I obviously had no idea that the nerves were responsible for the pain. He also proceeded to explain how the nerves worked, in layman's terms, so that I could understand. The caution was that if I was in any doubt, then don't touch! Something that stood out in his advice was the fact that the mind and brain control the spine and nervous system. Without them nothing else in the body can work. I have always remembered his words to me and his advice had a large impact on my future work. In fact I would consider his advice to be the most significant in my healing career.

I had several experiences of giving people a massage and then being told that as soon as my hands started to rub on the affected area, the pain would disappear! I began to realize that Mr. Martinovich had instilled in me a desire to learn more about psychic healing. While I did not really know anything about the practice, it had become obvious to me that I did indeed have some kind of healing gift that could help people and that I owed it to myself to explore further. After doing quite a few healings I began to develop quite a following in the area that I was living in. People who had heard what I could do came to see me. Some would ring first but others would just arrive on my doorstep. I never did mind, but I was always amazed at how quickly word spread. I began to mix with some similarly interested circles of people with the idea that maybe it could explain my gift of healing and why I was able to relieve pain so easily. Although the government frowned upon anything psychic or unnatural, it was never difficult to find people who had knowledge and experience in this area. There were publications around even then that could lead you to like minded people. I was certainly pleased by this, because I could begin to satisfy my own curiosity and make sense of what I could do that other people perhaps could not. Imagine my shock when I was told that I actually was a medium and not a healer and that energy was sent through me to the patient. This was something else to ponder – my life was certainly becoming quite extraordinary. I attended more circles and began to believe that I did in fact have guiding spirits with me. Let me digress for a moment. At this point I was still in my early 20's. I had discovered that I possessed an amazing gift and upon reflection, I realized that I had suffered no sicknesses or diseases throughout my lifetime. I mentioned this fact at one of the circles I was attending and was told that my Healing Spirit must have been with me since birth. Later, I was to learn more about this subject. I have never promoted myself as a healer, however, it seems that word of mouth is the best method of having people come to me for healing. People with sore backs, stiff necks, muscle pain and many other symptoms seem to make a track to my door. This has occurred in all of the numerous places that I have lived. I have never asked anyone for money for healings that I carry out, but rather I suggest that if the patient is satisfied with the healing, then they can leave a donation if they so wish. There is no expectation to do so and this allows people who come for healings the choice to donate. I have never refused anybody who has wanted my help and I would never make the excuse that I was too busy to assist anybody who needed the healing touch that I offer.

One night while sleeping, I seemed to sense a misty vision pass before my eyes. It was nothing that I could describe adequately - just a cloud like form that left me with a feeling of peace and contentment. I also had a tingly feeling down the left side of my face at this time which seemed like a message that my spirit guide was with me and that when I felt the tingling, I was to sit quietly and meditate. On doing this, I found that I would receive a message telling me what I had to do. Also I was told that instead of saying "I am healing," I was to say, "we are healing." After this experience, I knew that in fact that I did have a Healing Spirit and a Healing Guide assisting and guiding me at all times. From that moment on I had an amazing new insight. When a person asked for help, I somehow knew exactly what the problem was, where to treat and why the healing had taken effect.

I now began to attend classes where I could learn more about the meditative state and how to use this state in my healing. Before embarking on this I knew very little about meditation. I had heard the term and had a vague idea what it entailed, however I didn't realise that it would become such an integral part of my life or such a vital tool in my role as a healer. My first experience with meditation was definitely a revelation for me. I followed the directions of the guide and remembered them so I could use the practice myself. As I started to meditate more, I became aware of just what a valuable tool it was and what I could do with it. It was during an early meditation session that I had the most exciting experience. I had been asked to lie quietly and meditate and was directed to go to my haven - my place of retreat - where I could find solitude. I was then guided through a series of places. I did not know who was guiding me at this stage, but I assumed it was my Healing Spirit. I was then asked to imagine that I could see a picture of my last patient. A large screen appeared before me and on it was a picture of a lady. As I looked closer, I felt my eyes drawn to the area that we had previously treated. When I looked at this area (her knee), I found that there was a swelling behind the kneecap. I imagined my hands moving to this spot and the swelling disappearing almost instantly. I was then asked to dismiss the image from the screen and to dismiss the screen as well. All of it was gone and I found myself back in my haven. Moments later I awoke to find myself on the couch within the circle of people that I was learning with. I then related my experience to the group and was advised to get in touch with the lady in question. On doing so, I was told that in fact she had woken that morning with a sore and swollen knee, but now it was all right. There was no more pain or swelling.

That experience was another milestone in my healing experiences and I had another item to ponder. The event of the previous evening was clear in my mind and I began to wonder who had guided me through this meditation. Also, I asked myself how it was possible to heal someone's knee without them being there. To get an answer to these rather amazing questions, I again went into a meditative state. During this meditation a message came to me that absent healing was possible. Also I was guided to reflect on what I had been taught by the Aboriginal elders in Port Hedland when I had lived there. According to what they had taught me, and what I believed, thought transference was definitely possible. Using this knowledge, it seemed there was no reason why I could not send an absent healing to a person. It was certainly something to be very excited about.

I spent a lot of time practicing this method of healing. In some cases the healing was successful and in other cases, it did not appear to work. I decided to find out why the people I had sent healing to had not received it. At this stage I could not ask other people (apart from our circle) about this form of healing. The medical association and the government still frowned on this subject and it was certainly not an acceptable topic of conversation. However, I still sought an answer and the conclusion was that you have to get permission to send healing. It you do this, it will work as the patient was ready to receive the healing. If no permission is given, then the patient will not receive it. This permission does not necessarily have to come from the patient themselves, however it is certainly preferable, but not absolutely necessary. I can ask a family member for permission and if they believe that my healing will help the person in question, I will then do so. As I became more experienced in psychic healing, I also learned more of its complexities.

I continued to have people come to see me seeking healing for all different parts of their bodies and I was always amazed at just how effective word of mouth worked as a form of advertising for my services. Even though I was young and relatively inexperienced in the field, the number of people recommended to me gave me confidence in my abilities. I certainly never proclaimed myself to be the best, but it was always humbling to hear that other people held my skills in such high esteem. The back area seemed to give the most frequent problems amongst my patients. A young man came to me and told me that his doctor had diagnosed him with whiplash and was told to go to a physiotherapist, but as he could not find one, he opted to see me. My hands were guided to the left side of his neck and after placing a hand on each side of his neck, I gently began to massage. Healing energy in the form of heat was given and I felt a small lump on the left side of his neck whereby I was guided to put slight pressure in this area. I felt a click while massaging and the lump disappeared. After another minute of massage, the man told me that the pain had disappeared. He demonstrated that he could move his neck in all directions without any pain whatsoever and when he returned to see me a few months later, he was still pain free.

On another occasion I was visiting a country town. As was often the case, my reputation as a healer had preceded me and I carried out some work while I was there. A young lady came to me and asked if I could fix her knee, as she had to play in the final of her netball competition that night. On examining the knee, it looked to me as if she had 'water on the knee'. After massaging the knee for a few minutes, I was guided to apply some healing energy. I placed my hands on each side of her knee and transferred my thought energy. A minute or so later, she told me that the pain had gone and the swelling had lessened. This really was amazing because I could actually see the swelling diminishing before my eyes. I massaged for a moment longer and when I finished the swelling had gone completely. The lady thanked me and left. After such events like this, I take time to thank my Healing Spirits. The word thanks did not seem enough for the wonderful healings that I had been guided to perform. During a meditation that evening, I received a message that the spirits were indeed satisfied. This satisfaction was felt not by the word thanks, but rather by the sincerity in the voice and the action of the patient. The next day the lady came to see me and displayed that her knee was quite normal and pain free.

Healing from the Heart and Mind

CHAPTER TWO
<u>Growth through Experience</u>

My next trip in 1965 was to Port Moresby and I had been performing healings for a number of years, as well as working at my 'day' jobs. After leaving Perth Hospital, I had trained as a cook and had been working in that field for several years. I had originally gone to Cairns for a holiday but after three days, decided that I would like to have a look around Papua New Guinea. I arrived late one afternoon for what I believed would be a month long holiday. When registering at the hotel, a requirement was to give your Name, Address, Occupation and length of stay. I filled in all the details and gave my occupation as a cook/caterer. The next day I was asked to go to another hotel and see the manager. When I arrived there, I was asked to take over the chef's position as they were very short staffed. Also, I was asked if I would take the job of trainer/first aid for the hotel football team (Rugby Union). I accepted both positions. The chef's job was easy. I had two local boys to do my bidding, carry the groceries when shopping and assist with many other chores. The football ground was close to town and on training days, I was kept busy with massaging and the usual cuts and scratches that are part of contact sports.

On one occasion, one of the players came to see me about his sore lower back and a limp. I asked him to lay face down on the massage table and after massaging his back for a short time I was guided to his feet. I noticed that one leg was one inch (2.5cm) shorter than the other. Amazingly, my next action was something I had never done before, yet it seemed the right thing to do. I was directed to lift the short leg and pull and flick at the same time. The patient told me that when I did that, he felt a click in the lower back area and the pain went immediately. When he stood up he had no limp and no pain. This man was a Police Officer as well as the best football player in the team. He was well respected on and off the field by the players and public alike. My houseboy Jimmy told me the following day that I had been spoken about by the natives. The general consensus seemed to be that I was considered equal to their Witch Doctors. Given the status of the Witch Doctor in tribal society, this was to be taken as quite a compliment.

Instead of returning to Australia after my one-month visa ran out, I was asked to stay for the whole of the football season. The day after the grand final (which our team won), I was approached by the customs officer and was told that as my visa had expired I should get the next plane back home. This was quite amusing really since they had been prepared to overlook me overstaying my visa while I helped the team win, but once the grand final was over, it was business as usual for the customs officer!

Arriving back in Brisbane from PNG, I lazed around for a few days before boarding a plane for New Zealand. When I arrived in New Zealand, I immediately secured a position as a cook and, not surprisingly, I joined the local football (Rugby Union) team. This had become quite a tradition for me by now but it was something that I genuinely enjoyed doing. I was kept busy with the usual run of cuts, bruises and sore muscles and was also utilized as a masseur. Most of the players needed a rub down after training and also prior to a game.

One evening after training, I was called to the kitchen where a worker had just scalded himself. Apparently he had been putting live crayfish into boiling water and while dropping one cray into the pot, the tail of the cray scooped up boiling water all over his hand and arm. I immediately put my hands around the arm without touching and began to draw out the heat. I applied this method over the hand also and in three minutes there was no sign of a burn or scald. The redness had gone and the pain had subsided. The other workers in the kitchen were absolutely amazed. They had witnessed the incident and knew that the water was boiling. They couldn't believe that a burn could be treated so effectively and so quickly without any kind of medical assistance. The next day showed no sign of any scalding, blisters or redness on his hands and he could carry out his duties perfectly normally.

At this time, I found that my methods of treatment for pain were not the only way. I witnessed a man (who was a healer) sitting at a table with an assortment of coloured wool. This wool was cut in three-inch (7.5cm) lengths. He asked his patient to take six pieces of the wool, without him seeing which colours were taken. He was told to go home and line up the wool on the table. The next morning the healer phoned the patient and told him which order the colours were in - 1st, 2nd, 3rd, etc. and then the healer told the patient which colour was healing which part of the body. The patient reported back that he

Healing from the Heart and Mind

felt a lot better and that all pains were gone. I am always interested to hear about different methods of healing and have no doubt that different healers have success with a variety of methods. However, I generally find that my methods work best for me and I also believe that my healing spirits will always guide me to use the most effective way for each particular patient.

A man came to see me after being discharged from hospital. He told me that he had been unloading a truck of concrete into a skip, which would then be lifted to an area to be spread. At the time of his accident, he had filled the skip and then turned to clean the chute. As he did so, he was hit on the back by the skip. The force knocked him to the ground severely marking his upper back. He was taken to hospital, where he stayed for 3 days. When discharged, the doctors told him to consider himself very lucky that he had not been cut in half by the accident and was also told that there was no permanent damage. When I examined him, there were three discs that I felt were out of place. I began a quick meditation and then started to massage the affected area. My hands were guided to the relevant area. As soon as the heat subsided, I was guided to put pressure on the area between the shoulder blades. I distinctly felt some clicking and knew then that the discs had returned to their rightful place. The man got off the massage table and after moving his back sideways and forwards, he claimed that there was no pain whatsoever.

At the next meeting of our circle, I was asked if it was possible to do a healing inside the chest area. As I had never done this type of healing, I told the group that I would meditate to see if this was possible. Although I went to these gatherings to learn, inevitably I found that I was often the one doing the teaching. It was always humbling to accept the position of teacher, given that I still felt that I had a lot to learn. Perhaps the most important thing was that it was a sharing of knowledge.

At the next meeting of the circle, I asked the group if they were willing to allow me to put them into a deep meditation and then show them how to do an internal healing. They all agreed. I began by having the people completely relax and then to go to their haven to find their solitude. I also asked them to imagine that they could see a large screen in front of them and to put a picture of their patient on the screen. Next, I directed their attention to their heart chakra and asked them to imagine a shaft of pure green light coming from their heart chakra and to imagine attaching it to the heart of the patient on the screen. Next, they were to imagine a shaft of pure indigo light coming from their third eye and to attach this beam of light to the heart chakra of the patient also. I then asked them to take a deep breath and relax completely. As they relaxed, they would find that they were drawn closer to the screen. Another deep breath and then they would find that they were inside the image on the screen, standing between the lungs. They were then guided to relax further and then to begin to explore the lungs. The lungs should be of a uniform colour and dirty or muddy discoloration would mean there was a problem. After a few minutes of looking at the lungs, I asked them to go to any area that had a dark or muddy shade. I then asked them to imagine that they had scraped this area down and to apply a special ointment. As soon as this special ointment was applied, they would see the area grow new tissue, which would match the rest of the lungs. I then asked the group to imagine that they were now back to their haven and to dismiss the patient and then also dismiss the screen. All should now be gone.

I then asked them to imagine a shaft of pure sunlight descending and covering their whole body. This sunlight was to put energy back into their own bodies before returning to the now. I asked them to accept this sunlight for another minute and then to return from their haven and be back in the now. After a short break to allow the group to realize what they had done, I asked them, one at a time, to describe what they had accomplished. Their stories were similar. Some expanded more than others, but they all agreed that they had in fact done a healing. Although none of the group had ever done anything like this before, they were all excited and asked that I guide them again at the next meeting.

I had been in New Zealand for some time when I had an opportunity to take up a position in Queenstown. After driving through some of the most spectacular scenery in New Zealand, I arrived in Queenstown. The position of a cook in a hotel on the western side of Lake Wakatipu gave me a perfect opportunity to see some beautiful sunrises. The sun coming over the top of the snow-covered Remarkables Mountains was as beautiful a sight that I had ever seen. The whole of Queenstown in 1967 was really just a sleepy hollow. The full tourist boom was still in its infancy. The ski fields were attracting skiers and the outdoor skating rink was in full swing. As always, I was caught in the middle of all this action, attending to sprains, twisted ankles, bruising and any other miscellaneous injuries. A particular incident happened about six weeks after I arrived. The tourist Jet Boat that operated on the Shotover River was very popular and a slight accident left a lady with a lower back problem. At this point, I had been studying back problems since 1960 and had gained a lot of knowledge. With the help of my Anatomy and Physiology book and my healing guide, I had the confidence to apply the correct amount of pressure to the sore areas. In this case, I had three areas to apply pressure to. I did this and within 20 seconds, the lady was able to bend and twist without any discomfort.

I began a circle of meditation with a few friends and began to further my interest in internal healing. Explaining this method to the circle started to excite them as none had experienced or heard of this way of healing. One of the group stated that a friend had a circulatory problem and asked if this method could help. The problem was in both legs and had the appearance of varicose veins. The patient gave us permission to try this and made herself comfortable. The members had asked if I would lead them through each step. I began by having the group go into a deep meditation and relax in their haven. When they were all relaxed (I checked this relaxation by noting their breathing and posture), I then asked the members to imagine they could see a path in front of them. I told them to walk down this path; to note the flowers on each side of the path, the green grass and the tree branches overhead with the sunlight streaming through. As they followed this path, they were to imagine that they could see another path to the right. They then had to follow this path until they could see a sandy beach and told them to make themselves comfortable sitting on the sand. They were to note the small ripples of the water, smell the sea air and to feel the warmth of the sun that did not burn, but gave healing energy.

I continued on: "Now that you are completely relaxed, I want you to imagine you can see a large screen in front of you and to see an image of the patient on the screen. Take a deep breath and relax further. You will now feel a sense of love and compassion comes over you. I want you now to focus a ray of green light coming from your heart chakra and to send this ray of light to the heart chakra of your patient. Next, I want you to concentrate on your third eye. Send a ray of indigo light to the heart chakra of your patient. Now I want you to relax and begin to feel yourself drawn to the patient. You will begin to get closer until you find that you are standing inside the patient's chest and can see the lungs. I want you to take some time and examine the lungs. Notice that they are of a uniform colour - the texture is the same all over. Just make yourself comfortable looking at the lungs, as you will then be able to see the rest of the insides."

"I now want you to take a deep breath and as you exhale, I want you to imagine that you are at the main artery at the top of the leg. Now I want you to imagine that you have a small boat and that you are now inside the artery. We are going to clean out this artery. To do this, I want you to imagine you are moving in your boat, going down the leg. As you progress you will see some blockages. I want you to break up these blockages and to put all the broken pieces in the boat with you. Keep going down the leg and every time you come to a blocked area I want you to clear it. You will find it gets easier as you go along. Keep moving down the leg until you come to the ankle and then if all is clear, turn around and go back up the artery. Any small pieces that you did not clear on the way down the leg, please clear now. You will also notice that the blood is now running freer down the leg, indicating that there are no obstructions. When you get back to where you started I want you to drag your boat out of the artery. You will then notice that the artery will seal itself. Now take all of the broken pieces out of the boat and put them in a bin. Make sure that you close the lid. Imagine you are inside the artery of the other leg, follow the way down the leg and clean it out in the same manner as you did with the other leg. Do not miss any obstructions, as this will now allow the smooth passage of blood flow. When you feel that you have finished, I want you to return to the starting point. Now unload your boat into the bin and close the lid. I now want you to take a deep breath and as you exhale, you will find that you are sitting on the sand in front of the screen."

To finish the experience I instructed the group to dismiss the image from the screen, then dismiss the screen. All is gone. "Now proceed to your haven so that you may relax. To relax I want you to imagine that a cloud of white mist is surrounding your body. Watch as the aura takes the white from the cloud and puts the white into your body. You will instantly feel relaxed. On the count of three I want you to leave your haven, and come back to now.... 1...2...3 you are returned. Rest for a minute or so until you are relaxed, then we will discuss what each of you has achieved."

Healing from the Heart and Mind

I am always amazed at the way each member of the circle approaches the task of healing. Although each is given the same directions, they somehow vary and go about the healing in their own manner. Each of the group were delighted with their experience and asked me to take them through another healing experience. The patient we did the healing on came to our circle a week later and showed us her legs. There were no sign of lumps in the artery and the deeper purple marks had gone and the pain also had gone. The lady was very appreciative and wanted to join our circle. Although I was convinced that my healing guide did the healing and that I was the medium for healing, the members of the group were not quite convinced that they also had healing guides. I told them that at the next meeting I would show them how to find their healing guides.

After leaving Queenstown, I travelled to Wellington, which is the capital city of New Zealand. At the time, I was experiencing some pains in my chest. Now, I have on some occasions been able to heal minor ailments of my own, but I was unable to get any relief at this stage. I went to see a local doctor as I had not, as yet, met any healers in Wellington. The doctor had me admitted to hospital that day with a serious bout of pancreatus. I was in extreme pain and although I had tried to call on my healing spirits, I found that I could not contact them. Two days passed in a blur, then a most amazing thing happened. I felt as though I was floating in a mist of milky blue. I was floating along a passage, which then opened into a huge void. I now had no feeling of pain and it had been replaced by serene happiness and my anxiety replaced by calmness. Then I felt a cold breeze across my right shoulder and a voice called "hang in there". Immediately I was wide awake. A nurse was at my bedside and her hand was on my shoulder. I asked her what had happened and she told me that she thought I had died. That was when she called "hang in there".

The nurse was astounded that as soon as I awoke and/or returned, I stated that I had no pain or discomfort. I felt completely refreshed. On reflection, I found that the trip on that milky cloud was the most comfortable I had ever felt. No worries, no pain, complete freedom and.... How can one explain peace? When I had returned, I explained these feelings to the nurse, who then called the doctor and explained her version of the past few minutes. The doctor was skeptical, which I had learned was the norm for medical practitioners. The following day I was discharged from hospital, having refreshed my body with healing energy. One other aspect of this experience will always stay with me. The peace and comfort I felt at the time gave me a positive attitude about death and after this time, I was not afraid of dying. When my time comes to pass on, I know that I will look forward to peace.

It is pertinent to ask why I could not heal myself during this illness. As a healer, I cannot heal myself, although as stated above, occasionally I have been able to get relief from minor complaints. My gift does not work that way. My healing gift is a service to others and so if I need to be healed, then I must seek out another healer to help me. That is why people cannot be trained as a psychic healer if their only desire is to heal themselves. They must have a desire to help others and use their gift in that way.

I spent a year in Wellington and became involved with rugby clubs. I even had the opportunity to rub down some members of the All Blacks Rugby Union team. I soon found myself in the swing of things in this new city, attended some circles and met some lovely people. I would have to say that I never found it difficult to meet people with psychic awareness, no matter where I travelled. At the same time, however, I felt that I was getting restless and home sick. It was 1978 and I had been away from Australia for a long time and looked forward to returning home. My wife Gloria and I arrived back in Queensland and soon settled back into Australian life again. In this time some of Gloria's family also moved to Queensland. We stayed for a couple of years before travelling back to Perth, Western Australia where my family welcomed us back and had a house waiting for us. I had work as a cook at a large sailing club and continued with my healing when I was called on. I naturally made my way to the Palmyra rugby club, where I had started so many years earlier. The place was the same and the injuries were the same, but the people and the players were now different. I had certainly learned much more about healing and my own gift in the time that had elapsed.

CHAPTER THREE
Past Lives and Rugby in England

Several years later, I inherited a substantial amount of money and Gloria and I decided to go to England to see her sister, whom she had not seen for 23 years. This was to be a surprise for her 50th birthday. Also, I had heard that Devon was a very special and spiritual place. We arrived in November 1984 without realising or given any thought that November in England was the beginning of winter. Torquay in Devon was a beautiful place and we spent a lot of time walking around the churchyards and were surprised to see that most headstones had been removed from the lawns and placed along the fence line. This seemed to be common practice in the area as the churchyards were becoming crowded.

Three days after our arrival in Devon, I had a surprise visit by a newspaper reporter and a photographer. They requested they take a photo of me massaging one of their staff. I pondered on this. The next day there was half page on the back of the paper with the caption "Healing Hands Work on A Rugby Player." My brother-in-law showed me the paper and then admitted that he had phoned the paper and had organized the whole thing. That afternoon I had three phone calls, each from different rugby clubs. Of the three, I felt I should talk to one in particular as the father of one of the junior players had stated that his son needed to be 'built up'. I was invited to the Paignton Rugby Club to meet the committee and members and the next thing I knew, I had been appointed as the head trainer, physio and masseur. My wife and her sister had also discovered something that they had in common. They both had a yen for knitting machines.

With the rugby season just starting, physical exercise and massage was keeping me busy. I had started with 4 juniors to help build them up and by the end of the first week, I had the whole of the senior team and half of the juniors coming twice a week for exercise. Our first game was the reserve team who played the naval reserve team at Plymouth. The game was played at a brisk pace and our boys were lucky to come home with a win. The next week, our senior team went to a place called Mary Tovey on the Dartmoors Plain. The weather was freezing with sleet, rain and snow falling all at once. During the first half, the game suddenly stopped and the referee and a player were standing with their arms outstretched signifying a stretcher was needed. I ran out to the players and on the way I got a message of what was to be done. When I got to the injured player, I immediately sat the player up with his back to my legs. Then I lifted his legs behind the knees and pulled the knees into his stomach three times. I then pushed my hands as hard as I could into his stomach, behind the pelvis. I did this three times and after I had finished, the player got to his feet and the first thing he said was "there is no pain." The referee told me that a loose ball had been knocked into some players and one of the opposition players took a kick at the ball at the same time as our player ran in. The player was kicked in the groin so hard that his testicles were pushed into his stomach. It became apparent to me that this was why I was told to do what I did. There were no ill effects from the incident and the player finished playing the game, but while showering he noticed a large bruise. He informed me that the same injury had happened to him three years earlier and on that occasion, he had been hospitalized for just over two weeks before the pain had subsided.

Our next trip away was to Tavistock. The game was a quiet affair with no injuries and afterwards, the players headed for a Dungeon bar in town for celebratory drinks. I do not drink alcohol or smoke and the room was full of blue tobacco smoke, so I made my way out of there. I had a look around and I spotted a drawbridge. I was told that this was the Castle of the Duke Bedford. I browsed around and then saw a cathedral across a park. A plaque at the front of the building gave an account of the castle that had been constructed in 1308. One particular section on the front of the building really impressed me. The doorstep was made of oak and would have been eight feet long, two feet wide and two feet deep, when it was constructed. Looking at this doorstep properly for the first time, it was now completely different. It was still eight feet long and two feet wide, however the middle point had been worn away so much that it was now only two inches thick in the centre. To me, this represented thousands of feet had trodden on that doorstep. It was quite an amazing thing to ponder. As there was a service going on inside, I did not intrude.

I continued my walk around the area and felt as though I was being guided to a side street. Walking down this narrow street, I came upon a little church and entered the gate and found that all the headstones had been placed around the fence perimeter, like so many others in the same area. I walked to the church door and tried to enter, however, when I put my foot on the step, I found that I was being held back by some unseen force. I stepped back for a few seconds and then tried to enter again. The same thing happened. I backed off from the door and when I turned to move away, I noticed a large brass plaque on the lawn. This plaque would have been eight feet by six feet wide. I looked for an inscription, and all I could read was 1474. By this date it had been there for 510 years. As I was looking at this plaque, it seemed to move aside and I was looking into a hole. Suddenly one of the coffins moved out of the wall and a figure rose out of it and this person was dressed in an Army uniform. As I kept staring at this apparition he suddenly turned around and faced me. I received a shock as the face of the person seemed to me to be an image of myself. Except for the black beard, I thought I was looking in a mirror. The image then smiled at me and returned to his coffin and then the plaque returned. I returned to the door of the church and walked straight inside. This seemed to indicate to me that I had needed to get permission from the person I had just encountered, before I was allowed to go into the church. Once I got inside I saw that it was a very neat little place, which had five pews each side of the aisle. The most that could be seated at one time would be about 25 people. I was deeply shocked by this event and I was afraid that if I mentioned it to anyone I would have been certified. It wasn't the kind of thing that could easily be brought up in general conversation, but sometime later, I was to see a clairvoyant who would take me back to a past life.

Our next trip with the team was to London and I was the nursemaid to 20 members of the Colts team. We were to play a series of games with the Burnett Club. After settling into a motel we went to Burnett and were made most welcome. The first game was played with the usual bumps and bruises. They were quickly attended to on the spot and then forgotten about by the players who had been hurt. The evening dinner was a grand affair. We had a good meal, listened to the speeches and had a good laugh. Two particular young players were intent on having a good time and enjoying a few beers. They clicked their glasses together in a toast and unfortunately they hit the glasses too hard and one of the boys suffered a deep gash in his hand. I was called over to attend to the cut. I cleaned the cut as best as I could and then pressed the side of the cut together. I bandaged the hand and then the team manager took the lad to hospital. After the usual wait, a doctor looked at the hand and told the manger that he should have brought the lad to him as soon as the accident had happened and not a day or so later. The manager informed him that the accident had happened only an hour earlier. The doctor did not believe him and stated that, as the wound had already begun to heal, it was too late to put stitches in it. The hand was bandaged and the player was sent on his way. The cut healed completely within two days with no scarring.

At the end of the football season all clubs have a wind-up dinner and trophy presentation. Ours was a grand affair with about 350 guests and my wife and I were invited guests. At the end of the meal and before the speeches had begun, I was approached by a person whom I did not know. The people around me knew and respected this particular gentleman. He requested we speak in private. I was curious as to why I would be singled out for this conversation, but was soon to find out. With no preamble, he told me he represented the management of the British Lions Rugby Club, the most hallowed Rugby Club in England. He then informed me that the Lions Management would like me to accept a position as Head Physio at their club. I was amazed because trainers all over the world fought for this honour. I informed the man that my wife and I had just purchased our tickets to return home to Australia. I also mentioned that I did not have a Physiotherapy diploma. This did not seem to worry him and in fact, he assured me that something could be worked out. I then asked why he had selected me. He told me that all the referees submitted a report after each game in first grade rugby and my name had come up on a few occasions for being helpful in all aspects of first aid. I again apologised to him and told him that it was impossible to accept the position, although I was certainly honoured to have been asked. I also explained that I was overwhelmed and amazed to have been considered by him in that regard given his important position. We had already stayed much longer than we had first intended and knew it was time to leave. After 10 days of holidaying in Europe, we returned to Perth.

CHAPTER FOUR
<u>Healing Hands</u>

We arrived back in Perth happy to be home again, although we had enjoyed our trip away immensely. It didn't take long to settle back in and catch up on the many messages that had accumulated during our time away. Patients were soon ringing and calling around to see if I could help them. Christmas was approaching and I had promised a friend that my wife and I would look after their sheep station while they had a two-week break. The station was 386,000 acres in size. We soon arrived at Tuckanarra, 20 km. north of Cue. We settled in and I was soon shown the five different windmill runs. The longest was 285 km and had 11 windmills to check out. The shortest run was in the home paddocks which was a mere 48km and only four wells. I had to travel one run each day to ensure the windmills were working and that the tanks were full of water. It was an easy task and driving through the country area suited me just fine. On one trip, I took Herbie the Aboriginal Stockman with me, as there was some repairs that required two people to handle. On the way we stopped at a clearing and noticed a large circle of small stones on the ground. In the center of this circle, which has been cleared of all other stones and shrub, was a pile of five large stones. On the outer circle one small stone had been removed. Herbie told me that a group of five people had stayed there but had already left. They were now headed in the direction that the one stone had been removed from. There was another cairn of stones about 300 meters away but Herbie refused to comment on those.

Christmas Eve was soon upon us and our family, consisting of four adults and seven children, arrived. We were fortunate to have a garden at the station, with quite a lot of cabbages growing. Late that evening when all the smaller children were asleep, we took a lot of outer cabbage leaves and made a path of them to where the youngest was sleeping in her sleeping bag. We also planted a Cabbage Patch doll under a cabbage. In the morning we were woken with a scream of delight from the youngest. She came running into our camper van and showed us her Cabbage Patch doll. When I asked her where she got it from, her reply was "from the cabbage patch of course".

After Christmas dinner Herbie sat down and said there was trouble somewhere. He began to mutter to himself, then he would be quiet and then would mutter again for a long time. When he got up he seemed a little angry. I asked if there was a problem and he told me that some of the younger aboriginal boys had been drinking too much and had got into a fight and one of the fighters had been killed. Herbie then told me that he and some other Elders had made a decision that the one who hit the dead boy should be put in the Aboriginal gaol in Wiluna. This gaol was an area of hills that was patrolled by Aboriginal guards and their dogs. When a prisoner is sent to this area, he must find his own sleeping area and must also find his own food. The prisoner was also not allowed to take any spears with him.

I was grateful when the station owners returned some three weeks later and we could return to Perth.

We stayed around the city for a while and our circle restarted as it inevitably seemed to do. The numbers had now increased and they were on the lookout for new methods of healing to teach the other members. I was always willing to share any new methods or ideas that I had come across and others also contributed their own knowledge.

Some time later I received a note from one of my brothers stating that he had a problem with another bout of a recurring lung complaint. I went to see him to offer some help. Although we were close, he would not accept my kind of healing because I didn't 'give' him anything for his complaint. This is not an uncommon reaction to psychic healing. He had been a hard worker all his life and in the latter years he had been driving graders and bulldozers. All this work was done in dusty conditions and as a result, he had a lot of dust in his lungs. Previously he had suffered from tuberculosis, which had resulted in a hole in his lung. Now this affected lung was very weak. My brother was adamant that he did not want me to help him and I respected his wishes. It is frustrating for me when somebody refuses help but I accept that I cannot force them to be treated with psychic healing. I accept each person's beliefs and in such cases, I ensure them that I am available, should they change their mind.

It was now 1985 and my wife was getting a bit homesick for Queensland and so we began to ready our campervan for a return trip. Our van was actually a converted furniture truck that we had fitted out very well to suit our needs. I couldn't tell you just how many people I had treated in that van as we travelled around the country. We were in no great hurry and had opted to take the more scenic route across the top end of the country rather than going straight across the Nullabor Plain that was the most direct path. We headed to Darwin and on the way, encountered a hurricane as we approached Roebourne. This kept us off the road for two days. When we resumed our journey, we went to Port Hedland where I had begun my sojourn into healing. The town had changed in the time that I had been away. It was now the major port for the iron ore from Mt Newman. Some of the trains coming from Newman were almost two miles long and were pulled by five locomotives. It was certainly a far cry from the small settlement that had provided me with my first important experiences in the field of healing.

We moved on to Broome where we intended to refuel, stay the weekend and then continue onto Darwin. We booked into the caravan park and then took a walk through the streets. Broome was the hub for the pearling fleet and is the pearling capital of Australia. The luggers would come into Roebuck Bay, unload their catch of Pearl Shell, restock provisions and then return to sea with a minimal turnaround time. I met up with a man whom I had known in Perth. He was with the local football club. Naturally I was interested in the club after my many previous experiences with football and I went along to their first meeting of the year. The new season was beginning and as expected, I was appointed as the trainer/fist aid attendant. We decided that Darwin could wait as it would still be there when the football season was over. This seemed to be an enjoyable but temporary distraction. The first game was only two weeks off and training was held two nights each week. There were five teams in the Broome competition. One team was from Derby, two from Broome and also two Aboriginal teams. The latter teams were the ones to watch as they were fast and fearless. I immediately got involved with training exercises and body repairs. This time it was an Australian Rules football club, rather than rugby however, the training required and common injuries experienced by the players were pretty much the same. Outside the football club I soon had plenty of patients coming to see me with various ailments. Once again it didn't take long for my reputation as a healer to become known in the area, even though this was our first time living in Broome.

The first game of the season was on a Saturday and all concerned expected it to be a slow affair, but it was far from that. I was kept busy running out onto the field putting a plaster here, a bandage there and rubbing down bruised players. At the first break I had more rubbing (massaging) to do as the players did not begin training until two weeks before the first game. This meant a lot of sore muscles in the early stages until the players' bodies adjusted back to such hard physical workouts. When the game resumed and the play got a big more boisterous, I was called onto the field to attend to a cut eyebrow. The cut was the full length of the eyebrow and the bone was visible. I cleared up the blood and then I was directed by my spirits to run the ball of my thumb across the length of the cut. I did this and quickly noticed that the bleeding had stopped. I applied some ointment to the area and then liberally applied Vaseline over the whole area. The player resumed playing and at the half time break, I checked the cut and it appeared to be knitting together. I applied more Vaseline to keep the dust and dirt out and at the end of the game, the team coach told the player to see the local doctor immediately. When the doctor examined the cut, his reaction was that it did not require any sutures as the cut had knitted together quite nicely. He also mentioned that the player should have been to see him earlier when the cut first happened. Once again it occurred to me that the medical profession does not tend to believe when such amazing healings have occurred. This healing and the similar one I had done in England, made me wonder why cuts like these heal completely in half a day. They were both serious gashes that would have required stitches if treated by a doctor. I have yet to meet my healing spirits, but they are continually guiding me. I follow these directions without question and always find that their guidance is correct.

A few days later a friend asked me if I could babysit his children who were aged three and four and since I was not busy, I agreed. According to his mother, the three-year-old had a cold or something similar and was continually whimpering. I arrived at their caravan at 7.00pm and they said that they would be back by 10.30pm. The four-year-old was asleep and didn't wake the whole time I was there. I was sitting on the lounge and the three-year-old was lying near me, covered over. It was a warm night and I noticed that the child was sweating. I uncovered him and he then started whimpering. I was sure he was in pain so I put one hand on his shoulder to calm him. Within a minute, he appeared to be asleep. About an hour later I became thirsty. I got up off the lounge and was pouring a glass of water when the child began whimpering again. I sat on the lounge, put my hand on his shoulder and he immediately stopped the noise and went off to asleep again. Each time I moved my hand he would begin whimpering again. As soon as I replaced my hand on his shoulder the noise would stop. When the parents arrived home, both children were sound asleep. The mother commented that this was the first time in 24 hours that he had slept quietly. I then asked them to take notice of what happened when I removed my hand from his body. As soon as I did this, the child began the noise. I put my hand back and the noise stopped. The mother then picked up the child and he began whimpering again. She cuddled him, but to no avail. I put my hand on his shoulder and once again, the noise stopped. There was eye contact between the parents and a sort of bewildered look from the mother. I then told them that I had to get back to my place. I removed my hand again, took a couple of steps and the noise began. The next morning the parents came to see me to tell me that the child was in hospital in a serious condition. The doctor only described his condition as a fever. I went to the hospital to see the boy and he was worse than when I left the night before. The nurse was with me and as soon as I touched the child, his whimpering stopped. I stayed at the hospital for an hour to allow the child to get some rest. According to the parents after a series of injections, the use of an oxygen mask and nursing care the child was home in two days. The doctor could not tell the parents the nature of the illness, except that he may have been bitten by something to cause the fever.

The football season was in full swing and although I was kept busy with the team, I was still seeing other people. A carpenter/cabinet maker who did some work on my van came to me with a bad back. It constantly amazes me that people complain about the pain they are experiencing and put up with it for days before they come to get the ailment fixed when it usually only takes a few minutes for the pain to be removed. This chap was no exception. He hurt his back on the Monday and it was Thursday afternoon before he told me the pain was getting worse. I massaged the back for a few minutes, found where the problem was and within minutes the problem was fixed and the pain had gone.

Let me once again explain that I have no illusion that I am doing the healing. Without my healing and guiding spirits working through me, I am quite sure I would not be capable of doing this work. As a medium, I get a lot of pleasure knowing that my healing spirit has selected me for this work.

Two days after I had treated the cabinetmaker, I was called to the factory where he worked. I wondered how he could have another back problem so soon, but when I arrived he told me a story regarding his wife Jan. Apparently Jan had been so ill recently that the local doctor advised her to go and see a specialist in Perth. She was also very pregnant at the time. When she went to Perth, the first specialist examined her and was not too sure regarding her condition. Jan told him that she was losing her balance, had permanent ringing in her ears, her eyes were blurred all the time and she had a permanent headache. The specialist advised her to see his colleague in another area of town. The appointment was for the next day. On arrival at the specialist rooms, Jan told the same story and received a similar reply. They said they would take some blood for testing and that the results would be back the following week. The next day Jan was in the Maternity Hospital and gave birth to a wonderful daughter. The local doctor in the hospital listened to Jan's story and he thought Jan might be suffering from ME (Myallic Encyphacomyeutis). He said that he had seen the symptoms once before, however he said that he did not know of a cure. In the month that Jan was in Perth, she saw four specialists and the doctor in the Maternity Hospital. None of the medical people gave her any prescriptions that helped in any way. Panadol seemed to be the stock answer but it did little to relieve her symptoms. I saw Jan for the first time when her baby was 5 weeks old. As soon as I saw her I said "You will be better after two visits." I do not know what made me say that, but I guessed that I had received a clairvoyant message from my healing spirit.

I began by massaging Jan's shoulders and neck. While rubbing her neck, I felt that a disc was out of place and so gently applied a little extra pressure on the area and sure enough, a little click assured me that the disc had returned to its' normal position. I then gently massaged the optic nerves for 10 seconds. I then worked on the temporal area above the corner of the eyes for about 20 seconds. In all, I worked on Jan for no longer than 5 minutes. When I asked Jan to move her head she did so and exclaimed that her headache had gone. I made arrangements to see her again in two days time. This was to see if the headaches had returned and also to allow the eyes to refocus and for her balance to adjust. Upon returning, I found Jan at the sink doing the dishes and singing. I was amazed when she told me that I need not bother getting my massage oil out, as she felt that she was now completely healed. Jan thanked me and told me that she had slept soundly all night.

Bill's wife came to see me at the caravan park. Her husband had bent over to pull a tent peg out of the ground and while doing so had experienced a searing pain in the lower back. I was taken to their caravan park and Bill was on the bed lying on his back and had been there for two days. When I spoke to him, he said that he had been lying on his stomach for one day and needed to turn over. The pain was so bad that it took him two hours to get over onto his back. I then helped him back over to his stomach to examine his back. I noticed two large lumps on the spine that were very red and assumed that the pain was coming from that area. Gradual massage began to ease the pain. The healing energy that came through me helped and in about 10 minutes the severe pain had almost gone. I then began to manipulate the back so that the discs could return to the correct position. When I felt that the discs had in fact been put back, I began to gently massage again. Most of the pain had now gone but the area where the spine met the pelvis joint was a concern as there was still pain there. I told Bill that I thought he had put up with enough for the day and I would be back the following day. Bill was now able to stand and his first thought was to get over to the showers. The following day Bill was back on his bed with the only pain being in the pelvis region. I seemed to get a message to massage the area and then to adjust the leg joint and that would ease the pain. I did this and within five minutes Bill got up, walked to the steps, stepped down and turned around, walked back up the steps and declared himself better. He was now experiencing no pain whatsoever.

We received some disturbing news that my wife's mother had taken a fall off her 'nifty fifty' motor scooter and the foot stand had penetrated the calf muscle of her leg. Gloria decided the following day that she would get the bus from Broome and travel to the Sunshine Coast in Queensland. That night at 11.15pm the police woke me with the news that my brother had passed away in Perth. I decided to drive the 1800km back to Perth after seeing Gloria onto the bus. We arranged that Gloria would return to Perth in one month.

I arrived back in Perth and the necessary funeral arrangements were made. Once that was over, I began the job of sorting out his affairs. Our circle was glad to see me back in town. We began once again to learn through meditation. Each of us in turn would give an account of our accomplishments from the past couple of weeks. I recounted my experiences while in Broome. I was, by this time, very intrigued in the chakras and was learning as much as I could. Coupled with what I had learnt before, I now felt that I could talk on the subject of chakras. I was asked by the group to give them lessons, to advance their knowledge. I agreed and wrote a few pages on chakras. (See end).

Some time later a disturbing call came through to me that Gloria's mother was still in severe pain, even though it was some time since her motor scooter accident. We decided to return immediately to Queensland. When we arrived in Maroochydore in 1987, I immediately began the healing process on Mother's leg. Firstly I put my hands on each side of the leg calf muscle. I was able to feel the healing energy pass through me into the leg. As the energy warmed, the pain in the damaged muscles which had a deep hole caused by the footrest of the scooter, began to subside. I continued this type of treatment physically for about four days. Meanwhile, I used meditation to imagine the healing taking place in the tissues inside the muscle. By applying the thought process, I was able to see the new tissue growing on each meditation. Within two weeks, Mother was able to walk again without the use of a walking stick.

We had parked our camper van in a caravan park. One morning I saw a lady hobbling from the ablution block. It seemed that her right foot could not be put on the ground without it causing her pain and so my wife asked the lady to come in and rest. She told the lady who said she had sprained her ankle, that I might be able to help her. This lady was a nurse by profession and told me that two weeks rest would make the ankle better. I then asked if I could just rub the ankle with baby oil to ease the pain. She obliged and I began my work. Firstly, I was instructed to gently hold my hands each side of the foot and to gradually move my hands in a circular movement and then more pressure was to be added. Then I was to begin to use my fingers to feel the bones, the tendons and the swollen area. After what seemed like five minutes, I knew that the foot had no pain in it.

I asked the lady to stand up, but she was hesitant because she was afraid that her legs would not hold her weight. After I asked again, she stood, put her weight on the 'sore' leg and then stamped her foot. She looked at me and said, "there is no pain. I can twist my foot and there is no pain. How did you do this? I mean how can you remove pain?" I told her that my healing spirit removed the pain by sending healing energy through me. She remained there for a short while and I could see that she was debating the idea how I could have healing spirits. She then asked me if I could help her eight-year-old son who had a problem with bed-wetting. It appeared that she had tried all sorts of treatment to stop this problem including no fluids after 4.00pm and having him empty his bladder prior to going to bed. It appeared that as soon as the child relaxed and went to sleep, the accident occurred. I told her that I would visit her van that afternoon. During the day I meditated on the subject of the young boy and I soon knew what was to be done.

That afternoon I went to see the lady and told her my plan. The boy was brought in from playing and I explained to him that a nerve that controls the bladder was pinched in his back and this was the cause of his problem. I then asked the mother to lay face down on the bed and showed the lad the area where his problem was. He was ready for me to do this work as, in his words, he was ashamed to have a wet bed every morning. I had the boy remove his shirt and sure enough I detected a hot spot in his spine around the kidney area. After giving a gentle massage and a little pressure, there was a click that told me that the nerve had been released. I then assured the lad that he would not have his problem anymore and that he could go to bed and be sure to remain dry all night. Two weeks went by and the lady came to our van with a huge box of chocolates for my wife. There was a kiss on the cheek for me. She was delighted that there had not been a wet bed since.

Another lady passed our van each morning on her way to the showers. As she walked her right leg dragged and she limped badly, but she kept going without complaint. I asked her one morning about her problem and she admitted to having been diagnosed by the doctor as having Multiple Sclerosis (MS). The lady's name was Doreen and she had recently suffered an MS attack. I massaged Doreen's left leg for ten minutes and restored it from a very cold leg to normal temperature. When Doreen was sitting on a kitchen chair she could not move her leg or slide her foot along the floor without using her hands to lift the leg.

After checking her back and replacing three discs in the lower spine, I gave her a massage. After each massage there was a marked improvement and after a fortnight of treatment, Doreen was able to cross her leg over her knee while sitting on a kitchen chair. I continued treatment to help Doreen walk without dragging her foot. The process had taken two weeks and her symptoms had almost disappeared. I wanted to have another week of treatment but Doreen went on three weeks holiday. When she returned she informed us that she had suffered another attack of MS. However, she had decided that she did not want any further treatment and so I could do nothing more to help her.

In 1988 I took Gloria on a gem-hunting holiday to look for sapphires. We arrived at Tomahawk Creek in Northern Queensland and spent some time setting up camp, as we had planned on staying for about two weeks. There were five of us in the group and Gloria was the only female. I built an outdoor barbeque so we could cook our meals. I used some stones and packed earth around a thick steel plate. I was pleased with my efforts and decided that the next job was to gather firewood. The caravan and tents were all in place and our little campsite was looking good.

The digging for sapphires was progressing on the bottom of a creek bed. We had to dig, sift, wash and sort the dirt and debris and if we were lucky, we would come across a sapphire or two. On the fourth night of our trip, we were woken in the early hours by heavy rain. This didn't deter us from digging and in fact we were quite pleased as it meant that we could collect fresh water from the roof and there would be more water for washing the siftings. We were having a wonderful time and were also looking forward to a hearty meal after our days' work. Unfortunately our hunger would have to wait due to an awful accident.

Gloria had the fire ready, the barbeque plate very hot and the meat and vegetables ready for cooking. She approached the fire from behind as there was a breeze blowing light rain on the back of the fireplace. As she stepped on the slight rise of the fireplace, she stood on wet soil and as a result, her foot slipped and she fell. She put her hands forward to save herself and they landed on the red hot iron plate. Immediately she lifted her hands but then her foot slipped and her right arm caught the edge of the plate, just inside the elbow. There was a loud scream and we responded immediately. I was closest and first

Healing from the Heart and Mind

on the scene. I took Gloria to the tent and placed my hands over hers. The palms of her hands were white. The searing heat had burned the skin badly. By applying my hands to hers, I was able to draw a lot of the heat out of the burns. When I say 'draw the heat out', I do mean that I can genuinely feel the heat come from the burn into my hands. This heat doesn't burn me, but I can feel just how hot the burn really is. I gave her two Panadol tablets as a form of pain relief and continued my treatment on her hands. At this stage, I didn't realise that she also had a burn near her elbow.

For an hour, I continued to give healing treatment to her hands. When we stopped and looked at them, the burnt white skin had disappeared. Although the hands were still red, they looked almost normal. I then applied an antiseptic ointment very liberally over her hands and bandaged them. Dinner was forgotten for us, but I was able to get Gloria to sleep by using meditation. The next morning I was woken by Gloria telling me that her arm was causing her pain. When I looked there was a burn mark about seven centimetres long and one centimetre wide. The skin had broken and all I could see was a deep, burnt gash. Seeing this we decided to pack up and head back to Emerald, which was about 60km away. At the entrance to the turn off we knew there was black, boggy soil and we hoped that the vehicles would be able to get through it. A four wheel drive with a caravan went first and churned up a whole heap of mud. We went next in our Ford Falcon, towing a trailer. I put it in first gear and let it idle its way out. I will be eternally grateful that my Ford handled this task so well.

We arrived at Emerald Hospital and the doctor immediately applied a special ointment and hinted that a skin graft would probably be necessary. The others stayed at Rubyvale to continue their digging but we decided to head back home to Maroochydore. Although Gloria wasn't complaining about her arm hurting, I could see that she was in pain. When we arrived back home, we immediately went to see our own doctor. He pronounced that the wound had been cleaned and that the ointment was healing the area very nicely. The wound did heal without any further complications and a skin graft wasn't necessary. However, Gloria still has a white scar inside the elbow to remind her of the sapphire hunt.

By 1990 we had settled into life on the Sunshine Coast. I took over some rooms in Maroochydore and decided to combine some minerals and crystals with my healing massage. Generally speaking, I am not a healer that uses a lot of crystals, but I do recognise that they can serve a valuable purpose in many cases. Now and then when I receive my message of healing, I am told that a crystal will assist a person. When this happens, I look for a crystal of an appropriate colour and have the patient hold it while the healing takes place.

This message came to me when I was treating Shirley who had come to see me when she was suffering from a migraine headache. Shirley explained to me that she suffered from migraines about twice a week on average and the doctors that she had consulted weren't able to do anything about it. This kind of pain can be very disruptive to a person's life, particularly on such a regular basis. The only kind of relief that she was able to get was from painkillers. It was obvious that Shirley needed treatment that would prevent the migraine from occurring at all.

I sat Shirley in a chair and began to massage her neck and shoulders. I felt healing energy going into her neck and shoulders in the form of heat and then gradually put pressure on the disc in her neck. As soon as I felt and heard a click, I stopped massaging. I then explained to Shirley that I was going to massage the optic nerve for a few seconds. As soon as this treatment was finished Shirley got out of the chair, turned to me and confirmed that she no longer felt any pain. Something that had been causing her debilitating pain for long periods of time was cured in a matter of minutes and her great relief was obvious.

After her treatment, Shirley attended some of my healing classes. As she learnt more, she began to feel that she also had a healing spirit with her as she had relieved pain for some of her friends. Shirley eventually became a healer at the Spiritualist Church in Caloundra, Qld. She still refers people with bad backs to me, telling her patients "to see Ron, as he is the only one who will be able to help you." It is certainly very rewarding to know that I have played a part in somebody else discovering their healing spirit and subsequently using their gift to help others as well.

A short time later in 1990, an elegant American gentleman came to my rooms with his daughter who was suffering from a severe headache. This meeting was to have a lasting effect on my wife Gloria and myself. I asked the girl to sit on a chair and I began a healing massage on her shoulders and neck. I soon felt it was time to apply pressure to the point in her neck where I felt a disc was out of place. After applying a little pressure, the disc was back in place. I continued massaging for a short while and was soon informed by the young girl that the pain had gone completely. Once again this was accomplished in a matter of minutes as is quite normal in my less complex healings. Her father George was very grateful that I had cured his daughter's pain and was also fascinated with the minerals and crystals that I had. He informed me that his main interest was in opals and so I showed him a few that I owned. He purchased them off me and asked me to contact him if I was able to get any more. He was particularly interested in those that came from Lightning Ridge in NSW. He left his business card with me in the hope that I would be in touch again.

Another man I knew had suggested that I go to Lightning Ridge, mainly because the miners there were always having back problems and I would probably be able to help a lot of them. Travel was still something that I enjoyed and so I decided to take a trip down to The Ridge. It was a successful trip for many reasons. I managed to do some healings on the miners who were grateful to be freed of their pain. Given the nature of their work, it wasn't surprising that so many of them suffered back pain. I also purchased a lease on a mine and arranged things so that I would be able to travel down to The Ridge at least three times a year. This had all come about due to George's visit and his interest in opals. George later became a partner in the mine and our friendship continued. He has visited us on three occasions since our first meeting and Gloria and I have visited him and his wife in America twice. This certainly demonstrates how friendships can be formed in all kinds of places.

After discovering my own gift for psychic healing so many years ago, it is perhaps not surprising that I have often been asked to teach people the art of healing. In 1990, I decided that I would run such a course. A group of interested people was formed and classes began. I am always happy to share my knowledge, just as others helped me when I first became aware of my gift. I would estimate that over the years I have probably taught about 1000 people in the field of psychic healing.

I began by instructing the group to go to their 'haven'. When they got there, they had to relax and await a message. This message could come in a number of forms – as a feeling, a touch, an awakening, a vocal message or a vision. All sorts of messages can be conveyed to those who are seeking to heal others. A person who only wanted this gift for commercial purposes, rather than the desire to genuinely help others, would find that they couldn't perform a healing.

The selected group began a five-week course with sessions twice weekly. There was an hour of tuition and a lot of time spent on questions and answers. Each of the students in turn would act as the patient, while the rest of the group would see if they could find what the problem was. Obviously the 'patient' would not disclose their complaint until the session was over. It was very rewarding to see people discovering the wonder of healing. This course in particular stands out in my mind because there were a couple of people in the class who were extremely talented in the psychic field. They went on to succeed in several psychic fields. Although anybody can learn about psychic healing and everybody can benefit from learning how to meditate, it is true that the gift of being a psychic healer is very rare. I can recognise almost straight away if a person has the gift. It is also fair to say that a certain percentage of the people who have studied my course have done so just as another interest or hobby. While I would certainly never refuse to teach anybody about healing, it is important to remember that psychic healing isn't something that you can just master like other hobbies.

Like all aspects of my healing, these courses were never advertised and yet somehow word of mouth would have at least ten people enquiring about the next course, often just after the last one had finished.

People will sometimes ask about my own credentials and I will freely admit that I have no 'formal' qualifications in psychic healing. How can I have? Although times have certainly changed in the last 50 years and people are now much more open-minded, this kind of healing is still viewed with great skepticism. No university or other place of advanced learning offers training in any field of psychic healing. With all the experience I have gained over the past 50 years, I believe that there would be very few people who could test my knowledge or teach me things that I don't already know. I don't mean this in a boastful way at all. I simply think that psychic healing is something that is very much a culmination of a vast range of experiences. Inevitably, the longer you do it for, the more you learn. After more than 50 years, I do genuinely think that I have learned a lot. I am thankful to the people who taught me along the way and hope that I have done the same for others.

CHAPTER FIVE
Emotional Transformations

One day in 1990 Ling and her almost seven year old daughter arrived to see me. I was initially curious about the reason for their visit but was soon to discover a story that I found absolutely horrifying. I was absolutely appalled that things like this actually happened. Ling's daughter, who I will call Mary, was caught in a web of circumstances that no child should ever have to experience. Apparently Ling and Mary were trapped in a sect of men who dominated females and abused them.

This is part of the story as it was relayed to me. On the night of a full moon, Mary was taken from Ling by her father and placed on an altar. When she was just three years old, Mary was undressed and the ritual began. There were twelve males present who were all in disguise. One by one they approached Mary and performed a sexual act on her. When each male had taken his turn, Mary was returned home to her mother. It goes without saying that the psychological and physical damage to the child after this ritual was extreme.

I had numerous questions to ask, but I realised that I would have to take things slowly. Ling was still extremely secretive about the sect and would only give the briefest outlines about what had taken place. Apparently Ling had been subjected to the same ritual every three years until the age of 15. She was extremely concerned about her daughter having to endure the same unspeakable horror that she had.

When I asked Mary about the event she could remember being hurt, but not how it had happened. The most obvious thing was that she had developed a hatred for men. It took me over two hours of cajoling and bribing her with crystals to get any response at all. Mary was becoming very sick, as she knew that on the full moon of the coming month she would be placed on the altar again. At this stage Mary would not allow me to get within three feet of her. If I put my hand out to her she would cringe and back away. After a discussion between the three of us, it was decided that I would put Ling and Mary into alpha/theta to try and remove the pain of the event that had happened almost three years before.

I began by having Ling and Mary go to their haven. When I felt that they were completely relaxed, I asked them to follow a path, which would lead them to a small pond and a small waterfall. I asked them to rest here and to get the feel of the water sprite that would give them energy. After they had relaxed (I could tell when their breathing became slow and regular), I directed them to a new path. This path led them to a building that had a lovely pale pink door. I asked them to enter through this door. They found themselves in a passage that was full of toys. On the walls they could see numbers which went backwards from seven to one. I then directed them to walk down this passage and explained that as they did so, they would become younger. When they reached number one, Mary was back to being a one year old. Then I asked Mary to remember what she did on her first birthday. Next I guided Mary to number two. On the way I asked her to remember all of the good times between her first and second birthdays. My next step was to guide Mary along the passage to the two and a half year mark and to have her remember what had happened until that point. The next step was to direct Mary to the three and a half year mark and to explain that there was nothing to remember from this time. The walls at this number did not have any toys or books on display. The whole area was empty.

I then suggested to Mary that on the way to number four she would have some good times. Her mother was with her every day and they enjoyed each other's company. Mary's fourth birthday was great with lots of presents and cards and all the girls gathered around. Her fifth birthday was similarly happy and fun. Then I directed Mary to her sixth birthday. I had her remember that her mother had a new partner who was a nice, kind man that would protect her. I told her to remember all the nice things that he does for her.

I then directed them to walk down to the door and then go outside into the fresh air. I told them to take a deep breath so they could relax and remember all the good things that had happened to Mary. I directed them back to the waterfall and the pond and told them that the water sprite would give them energy to return to their haven. I told them that on the path back to their haven, there was a small hut with an open door. They were not to be afraid as there were three wise men sitting inside. I told Mary to go to the door and that one of the wise men would give her a message. After she received this message I told her to continue back to her haven. I then instructed her and

Ling to relax, take a deep breath and relax even further. After instructing them to have a small rest I bought them out of alpha/theta.

I then asked Mary to tell me what she could remember of her trip. She had a good memory and could recall most things. The only part that she was unsure about was why she didn't have a party on her third birthday.

Ling made an appointment for two weeks later to see if we could work on convincing Mary that her dislike for all men could be changed.

Ling and Mary came back to see me two weeks after the first visit. After questioning Mary, I discovered that her dislike for men was as strong as ever. Ling asked if we could do the alpha/theta treatment again. This time I approached the problem in a different way. I put Ling and Mary into alpha/theta and when I felt they were relaxed, I asked them to follow the path down to the beach. Here I asked them to relax again and then to imagine that they could see a movie screen in front of them. When they were fully focussed, I asked them to imagine that they could see a picture of themselves on this screen. When they had done this, I asked them to imagine that they were being drawn to the image. I then told them to imagine that they were inside the body. When I asked them to think of the brain, I knew that they would instantly find themselves there. Next I asked them to imagine that the brain was divided into three sections and in each section there are markers. I told them to match up all these markers; some were black and some were white. I explained that some would be in clumps of three or more but they had to make pairs of one black and one white marker. Any that were left over had to be discarded. I told them to do this in each section and that when they were finished they would have balanced Yin-Yang, which is the positive and negative of the human mind.

I then directed them to imagine that they could see a shed at the back of the garden (brain). I told them to go to the shed and to open the door. Inside they would find phobias. Next I instructed them to clean out the shed and to sweep out the phobias and put them in the bin. I told them to close the lid when all the phobias were in the bin. Next I told them to clean the floors, walls and ceiling to ensure that there were no phobias left anywhere.

I then had Mary and Ling imagine that they were calling lovebirds to them. I told them that the birds would come and that they would go into the shed. Each bird had a message tied to its leg. I told Mary and Ling to stop a bird and to read the attached message. They would find that it was an affirmation. Next I told them that as they had balanced their Yin-Yang and had removed all their phobias, they were at peace within themselves. I told Mary and Ling to imagine that they were back on the beach and to dismiss the image on the screen and then the screen itself. Finally I directed Mary and Ling back to their haven and told them to rest there and feel the energy. I told them to replace the energy that they had just used. I then asked them to return on the count of three. As soon as they were able, I had Ling and Mary relate their experiences to me. All was normal and I was pleasantly surprised when Mary said "I now do not have any fear of these men. I am just going to tell them to go away and leave me alone".

This was a great relief as this little girl had suffered enormously and deserved a chance to live a normal life. I am pleased to advise that Ling and Mary had no further contact with the sect that had damaged both of their lives so horribly.

In 1991 I was called upon by a noted naturopath to see a patient of hers. This man had been diagnosed with prostate cancer and her attempts to heal his illness with natural medicines had been unsuccessful. The naturopath knew that I had assisted others with cancer to heal themselves. She felt that it was certainly worthwhile to see if I could help this man. I obliged and went with her to a home in Golden Beach, where I met Charles. He explained to me the chronology of his illness, his doctor's verdict and the usual kind of prediction that he had x months to live. I explained to Charles what I intended to do and then went to work on him.

I began the healing by having Charles take three deep breaths to relax his body. I then put him in a state of alpha/theta. After a short while I instructed Charles to imagine that he could see the prostate gland. I also asked him to note any discolouration of the gland itself. When I felt that he was comfortable with looking at the discoloured gland and noting the irregular small bumps, I instructed him to begin to scrape all of the discoloured parts away. After scraping each area, he was to liberally smear some special ointment over the area (he mentally took the scraper and ointment with him). Then he was instructed to put all the scrapings in the bin and to close the lid. He was to repeat this action several times, until he had scraped the prostate clean.

When I brought him back, I asked him to relate to us what he had done. Everything appeared to have gone to plan until I asked him if he had put all the scrapings in the bin. He said that he had knocked the bin over and just left it there. In my mind I could see all the cancerous pieces just lying around and this was worrying. I informed Charles that I would be back the following week to repair any damage that may have occurred. While discussing the healing with Charles and his wife, I discovered that Charles was quite worried about becoming a statistic. Apparently he had been told that the Government kept a record of people who died of a particular form of cancer e.g. women with breast cancer and men with prostate cancer. It was quite obvious that he did not wish to become a statistic. He then asked me to come back the next week and complete the healing.

When I arrived the following week, I found Charles to be in a very good state of mind. He was ready for the follow up session. Throughout the healing everything went to plan. The prostate was checked and looked to be in good order. The scattered scrapings were collected, put in the bin and locked. During the discussion afterwards, Charles assured me that his prostate was again normal.

Three weeks later Charles' wife phoned me and told me that Charles had died in his sleep. Apparently they both knew that Charles had advanced bone cancer, but had chosen not to tell me. His overwhelming concern had been to not die a government statistic and by healing the prostate cancer, he could no longer be counted as such.

A valid question perhaps is why I did not notice the bone cancer. In this case, Charles had only told me about the prostate and I concentrated solely on this area. I had healed what Charles wanted me to heal and that is all that I can do as a psychic healer. So rather than viewing this case as a failure, I would count it as one of my greatest successes.

Susie came to see me at 9.30am one Saturday morning. She wanted healing as she had an important date that evening. She had been thrown off her horse the previous day during some trails and the injuries were all facial. Her chin and nose were grazed and bruised and she also had quite a headache.

Firstly I massaged her shoulders and neck and located the disc that was out of place. This was put back with a little pressure. The optic nerves were then massaged for a few seconds to ensure that they were working properly. In a matter of minutes the headache was gone.

The next step was to work on the external injuries. Firstly I put one hand over her chin and the other hand behind her head. I was conscious of the energy that was being sent through my right hand and coming back through my left. This was putting the healing energy through the sore chin. I held this for three minutes and then changed my hand to the nose. I allowed the same procedure to heal her nose and then set to work on her forehead. As I began I noticed that the forehead was also bruised as well as grazed so I gently massaged the affected parts with both hands for about three or four minutes. I was meditating throughout this massage and during the meditation, I was imagining the bruises leaving and the grazing healing. I also imagined applying my special ointment that came from my healing spirit. It began to work immediately.

In less than 15 minutes the healing was completed and Susie was delighted with the results. There was no sign of bruising or grazing – the nose looked normal, the chin had no marks to show where the soreness had been and the headache had gone completely. Injuries that would have taken a minimum of several days to heal in normal circumstances had been cured in less than quarter of an hour under my healing touch. Once again I was in awe of the gift that I possess and how wonderful it is to help somebody.

Susie came back to see me again some time later after another fall from her horse. This time she had been competing in a cross-country race of 125 km. Apparently her horse had baulked at a log jump and she had flown over its head and landed on her backside. Suzi immediately got back on the horse, which was unhurt, and continued on with the race. At the next compulsory stop, Susie was beginning to feel very sore at the base of her spine. She was also experiencing pins and needles down her left leg. When it was time to remount and continue on with the next section of the race, Susie found that she could not climb back onto the horse. Much to her disgust she had to forfeit her position in the race. I saw her the day after the race and she was very stiff and sore. After I examined her, I decided that the main concern, apart from some bruising, was a very hot spot at the base of her spine. It also felt like her coccyx was damaged.

I began my treatment by applying healing energy. I did this by massaging the pelvic area and also the lower spine. This seemed to ease the pain almost immediately. I then went to her feet and found that one leg was about 2.5 cm shorter than the other. I gave the short leg a flick and pull at the same time. Her legs were now the same length again. I then went back to the lower spine and found that most of the heat had gone. After a little more massage and some pressure with the flat of my hand, the disc that had been out of place was soon back in its correct position. I also noticed that the massaging over the buttocks had removed some of the colour from the bruising. Susie fully recovered within two days of falling from her horse.

Liz came to see me one day, complaining that she had woken up that morning and could not turn or bend her head. Her neck was stiff and sore and said that she had not injured it in any way. It is easy for a disc to get out of position, even when a person is just carrying out everyday chores. Sometimes sleeping in the wrong position can do it. It is not necessarily something that is caused by an accident or other kind of physical injury.

I examined her and confirmed that the neck was very stiff. I began working on Liz by massaging her shoulders and down the back to below the shoulder blades. When all of these areas responded and became relaxed, I gently began to massage the neck. After two minutes the muscles relaxed and I was able to turn Liz's head. I continued to massage for a little while longer and then felt and heard a click. This told me that the disc had returned to its rightful position. After a little bit more healing massage Liz announced that there was no more pain.

Healing from the Heart and Mind

CHAPTER SIX
Confirmation from Spirit

One day in 1991 I had a visit from an American Indian called White Cloud. She lived in the popular resort town of Noosa and had been conducting a clinic there for a few years. As this was just a social visit, we were chatting about healing techniques when all of a sudden White Cloud stopped talking. Her eyes nearly popped out of her head and she pointed behind me. "Who are those two huge Mongolian looking men behind you?" she asked in surprise. I looked around to see whom she was talking about but I couldn't see anybody. White Cloud described the men in detail and as she spoke, I became aware that she must have been talking about my two healing spirits. I had named them Mr Wong and Mr Lee. I explained that I had felt their presence before but I had never seen them. Mr Wong and Mr Lee then seemed to disappear as quietly as they had arrived. I rarely see my healing spirits but I can often feel their presence. When I get a tingling sensation down the side of my face, I know that they are nearby. I don't know why I get different healing spirits from time to time, but can only accept what happens and thank them for choosing me as their medium.

Early mornings are a habit for me. At about four o'clock I get out of bed, have a shower and then go out into my shed in the back yard to meditate. One particular morning in 1991 (I should have noted the date), I had an amazing experience. I was deep in meditation when a picture of the Last Supper appeared on my shed wall. All the people in the picture were moving, eating and talking. Then from the back of the room a young lady who was wearing a toga approached me. She just walked out of the picture and stood in front of me! I was dumbfounded to say the least. With her arms outstretched and a tray in her hands she said "Master I have come to serve you". I replied that I am a healer's medium and that I am here to serve others. The girl replied "No, Master you are a healer". Then a voice from the end of the table caught my attention. I looked around at the figure of Jesus and heard him say, "you are a Master Healer". Then the picture and the girl faded and disappeared from view. I still reflect on this most extraordinary event and count it as one of the most memorable events of my amazing life.

CHAPTER SEVEN
The Challenges of Cancer

February 1995 turned out to be one of the most interesting months of my life. I received a phone call from a woman called Joan who worked as a nurse who asked me if I could come to her house at Golden Beach quite urgently. She wouldn't elaborate over the phone but I could tell by her tone that she was quite desperate. My wife Gloria and I were there within an hour and we listened as Joan explained her illness. She had been diagnosed by two leading cancer specialists as having two large tumours in the small intestine. It was obvious that she was greatly distressed and very frightened and for that reason, I wanted to begin work immediately.

I asked Joan if she was aware of the term alpha/theta. As she wasn't, I explained to her that the brain generates electricity. This electrical impulse creates pattern states in the brain, which in turn triggers off impulses to the nervous system. These patterns or waves are divided into four major categories – alpha, beta, delta and theta. Delta are the slowest frequencies and operate between zero and four cycles per second. These usually occur when a person is in a coma or under anesthetic. Theta operates at about four to seven cycles per second and usually occurs when a person is deeply relaxed or daydreaming. Alpha operates at about seven to fourteen cycles per second. Being in the alpha level benefits the physical body by establishing a renewing and self-healing process. Being under hypnosis or meditation accelerates this process. Beta operates at 14 cycles per second and higher. It is associated with alert, rational and analytical behaviour. The alpha/theta state occurs by combining affirmations and visualisations, which help to get a person into a deep meditative state. The breathing becomes deeper, the muscles relax and the eyes become unfocussed.

After explaining this to Joan, I explained that it takes about three minutes to get into the alpha/theta state. Firstly, I had to have her permission to put her into this state and also explained that for her protection, if I so much as touched her with my little finger, she would become instantly awake. Joan agreed to be put into alpha/theta. I began the process by having Joan take three deep breaths and when I felt that she was relaxed, I directed her to her haven, a place of retreat. When she reached there, I had Joan completely relax her body by doing more deep breathing. When I felt that she could respond to my directions, I asked her to imagine that she could see a path in front of her and to imagine that she was walking along this path and to see the flowers on either side and feel the sunlight filtering through the branches overhead. Next, I asked her to follow another path that branched off from the main path. This path would take her to a golden sandy beach. She then had to find a quiet spot where she could sit down and relax. I explained to her that the sunlight would not hurt her in any way and in fact, the energy from the sun would help her in her healing.

I then asked Joan to imagine that she could see a large screen in front of her and to imagine an image of herself on the screen. Next, I asked Joan to take some deep breaths and as she did so, she would feel herself being pulled closer to the image on the screen. On the third deep breath she would immediately find that she was standing between her lungs. As the tumours were in the small intestine, I asked Joan to imagine that she was in that area. I directed her to find the tumours and to begin to pull these tumours out by the roots. Joan was breathing normally through this session, then all of a sudden, she became agitated. She was moving about on the bed and I had no choice but to bring her out of the alpha/theta state.

We discussed what had happened and she explained to me that she had no trouble in following the directions to her haven or the beach. She had seen the screen and entered the body through her lungs without any problems. When she got to the small intestine, she had removed four small tumours, spread each area with special ointment and seen the new tissue grow. However she said that when she had touched one of the large tumours, the pain had become unbearable and she wasn't able to cope with it. That was when I bought her out of alpha/theta. Joan was relieved that she had removed four small tumours however, she thought she had seen some more small ones, as well as the two large tumours. We made arrangements to go back and see Joan in two weeks time.

Although I had other people come to me over the next two weeks, I kept thinking about Joan and the two large tumours. Then one day I was given the solution, it came to me during one of my meditations. When the day arrived to see Joan again, my wife was very excited as she predicted that we were about to see a healing that had not been reported before. My wife will admit that she has no ability to heal, however she can follow the healing and see all that goes on.

We arrived at Joan's place and found her in a very excited mood as she felt that something very special was about to happen. I immediately prepared Joan to go into a deep meditative state and she soon became calm and relaxed. It was very easy for her to follow directions this time and we were soon back in the area of her small intestine. I directed Joan to remove all the tumours that she then saw and to put some of the special ointment on the affected area. Then, without warning, Joan began to shudder. I immediately asked Joan to stop what she was doing and to relax and to then take another deep breath and relax further. Because Joan was a nurse, I began to give her the instructions that had come to me during the past week by instructing her to imagine that she had a spray can of anesthetic and to immediately spray the two large tumours. When she though that both were completely anaesthetised, she was to get the tool that was appropriate for removing the tumours. After about two or three minutes Joan completely relaxed and her breathing became normal. I waited for another minute and then slowly bought Joan back to consciousness.

When Joan opened her eyes she displayed the nicest beaming smile that I had ever seen and this explained everything. Joan profusely thanked my wife and myself and then told the most amazing story. Firstly she described in detail, her journey to the small intestine and spoke about the removal of four small tumours, about touching the largest tumour and feeling severe pain. Then to her surprise, a can of anesthetic appeared and after spraying for a short time, the pain was gone. She used a scalpel to remove the two tumours and then spread the special ointment liberally over the affected area. She was amazed that the new tissue grew so quickly and blended in so perfectly. During this discussion Joan made some very important statements. Firstly, she said that after the healing she was quite certain that she no longer had any cancer in her body. Her mind was completely satisfied that she was now clean. Secondly, she assured me that she would see her specialist to get a clearance from him. Joan said that her specialist had given her only three months to live and told her to get her house in order and by those calculations, she now had only twelve days left to live. To this statement I replied "No, you have the rest of your life".

We left Joan in a very good state of mind and explained that we were going to America on holidays for a month. As she was now convinced that she was totally cured, Joan said that she would contact me later to let me know how she was getting on. It was to be quite a while before I heard from her again, but she was always at the back of my mind. I had continually sent healing thoughts to her since our last encounter and hoped that she was doing well. We returned home from our holiday and got settled back into everyday life again. After clearing all the accumulated mail, I sat and listened to the tape on the answering machine. There were many messages, but none were from Joan. This absence of contact placed me in a real quandary. I had considered phoning her house but didn't quite know what to expect. What if she had passed away and her family condemned me for giving her false hope? Eventually I decided to sit quietly for a while and see if any messages came to me. I decided that not phoning her was the approach that I would take.

It didn't take long for the steady stream of patients to build up again. Before I knew it, four months had passed and there was still no word from Joan, although she was always at the back of my mind. Then one day I heard her voice at the other end of the phone line. My heart skipped a beat as she was obviously still alive and well and I was very relieved to hear her. Soon we got around to the purpose of her call in that her shoulder was giving her a lot of pain and she wanted me to see if I could relieve it. I made arrangements for her to visit that afternoon and made sure that there would be no interruptions while she was here.

When Joan arrived she gave Gloria and I a warm hug and began to fill us in on what had happened since we had last seen her. She explained how she had gone to see her local GP after the second healing session. He had checked her over as best he could and then recommended that she go back to the specialist who had given the original prognosis six months earlier. The specialists were apparently stunned to see Joan still alive and looking so well. They did every necessary test and took several blood samples. They also asked Joan to return in four days to discuss the results of the tests.

When Joan returned on the designated day, the senior partner gave her the results. He said "The news is great! You no longer have any cancerous tumours in your body and you must be pleased that you followed all our instructions to get better."

Needless to say, Joan was furious at this response. She didn't hold back when she responded. "You sent me home with just three months to live with no hope that I would ever get better. I went to see a psychic healer who cleared ten tumours and not the two that you had diagnosed and in just two sessions that took only two hours each."

The renowned surgeon didn't appreciate her response. He replied that the idea of psychic healing was ridiculous and that there was no such thing. He also said that the people who conducted it were frauds and it was a load of rubbish. Joan didn't take this from him. In her words, she gave him a serve like he had probably never received in his life. Her parting words to him were "Now you know that you are not God, or ever will be and you should also be more responsible and sure before passing out death sentences!!!"

This was the first time that I had ever heard Joan say a bad word about anyone. I put it down to anger, relief, despair and the secure relief that the three months had passed and she was still very much alive. I then took several minutes to calm Joan down and to take the pain away from her shoulder. Before she left, she asked if she could continue on with her ballroom dancing competitions. I explained to her that I couldn't see any reason why she shouldn't, as long as she didn't overdo things. I was to see Joan again, but not for quite some time.

It would be true to say that successfully treating Joan's tumours was indeed one of my greatest successes however, she is certainly not the first cancer patient to be cured in this way. Different healers may approach the problem in other ways, but essentially the idea behind the treatment is that the mind has great control over curing disease and   I will give you an example. Dr. Carl Simington and his wife Stephanie are leaders in the field of holistic health. They have been using visualisation and relaxation in their treatment of cancer since the early 1970's with well-documented results. The startling fact with their cases is the survival rate of the patients, which is twice that of the United States nations' average. Data was collected from 159 patients who suffered incurable cancer. Each patient was treated for a four-year period from 1974 to 1978. Sixty three of these patients were still alive after four years. Fourteen of them (22.2%) showed no signs of disease. Twelve (19.1%) showed that their tumours were regressing. Seventeen (27.1%) patients showed that their cancer had stabilised. Twenty patients (31.8%) showed no tumour growth. Given that all the patients had been told that their disease was incurable, the results are quite amazing.

The following case history impressed the Simingtons at the beginning of their work. In 1971 a patient, who had a type of throat cancer, came to them for treatment and was in a grave condition and had little chance of survival. He had lost a considerable amount of weight and was extremely weak. Before the cancer developed he weighed 130 pounds, but had since lost 32 pounds and at the time he came to them, his weight was 98 pounds. He could barely swallow and had difficulty breathing and had less than a 5% chance of survival beyond five years. The physicians who had been treating him were unsure if continued treatment was advisable since they considered his case hopeless.

Dr. Simington began treating the patient by explaining that success depended on the patient's active participation in his own treatment. He explained also that he himself had the power to influence the course of his own disease and then devised a program of relaxation, affirmations and visualisation. The patient was advised that three times daily he must set aside a period of approximately five to fifteen minutes for self-healing. This was to be when he woke in the morning, after lunch and at night before going to bed. During these periods, he was instructed to sit quietly and relax and to pay attention to the muscles in his body and to see them in a fully relaxed state. Once he was in the alpha/ theta level, he was to go to a place where he was perfectly calm and at total peace. After he returned from this perfect place of relaxation, he was to then visualise his cancer clearly in whatever form it took.

Dr. Simington then asked the man to visualise the radiation treatment he was undergoing as consisting of millions of little energy projectiles which bombarded the cancerous cells in its' path. Since the normal cells were stronger and healthier than the cancerous cells, the projectiles wouldn't harm them. However, the weaker cancer cells would be damaged beyond repair and they would die. In the final stage of this treatment, he was asked to visualise his body's white blood cells swarming over the cancer cells, collecting the dead and dying cells and carrying them off to the liver and kidneys where they would be flushed out of his body. He was also told to see the cancer shrinking in size in each successive meditation, until the cancer disappeared and his body returned to normal. The results of these combined radiation and visualisation treatments went beyond the Simington's expectation and anything that they had previously experienced in purely physical intervention. The patient made remarkable progress and he showed virtually no ill effects from the radiation treatment. Halfway through the treatment, his throat was so improved he could eat again. He gained weight and strength and his general appearance showed remarkable improvement and most importantly, the cancer had progressively disappeared. An important element of the Simington's treatment was instilling in their patient a sense of control of his disease. In the case just cited, the patient reported missing one of his visualisation sessions during his course of treatment. Interestingly, he told the Simingtons that he was quite upset about missing it because, by doing so, he felt he was losing control over his treatment and was afraid that it could hinder his ability to control his state of health. That patient continued his rapid progress under the Simington's care and within two months of beginning the treatment, there was no longer any sign of cancer. His firm belief that he could influence the course of his disease was made more evident when near the end of his treatment he said to the doctor "Doctor in the beginning I needed you to get well, but now I think you could disappear and I could still make it on my own".

CHAPTER EIGHT
More Success

One day I had a call from a lady asking if she could bring her nine-year-old son to see me. She explained that he had severe asthma and they were exploring all options to help him overcome it and the appointment was made for the following day. I have mentioned before that in healings, various types of tools are used to help cure different problems. My tool for this boy's condition was honeycomb!

The woman and her son, Rob, arrived promptly for their appointment the next day and I explained that whilst no cure had been found for the asthma germs, I was sure that we would be able to assist his breathing. Rob's problem was that it was easier for him to breathe in air than to breathe it out. I showed Rob my piece of honeycomb and explained that I would use this to help him breathe. He looked quite perplexed and so I explained how it would work for him.

I began by putting Rob into a deep meditative state. He was unable to breathe deeply and this made it more difficult to achieve the alpha/theta level. When we had Rob safely in his haven, I began by having him receive some healing energy. This was in the form of a ray of sunshine, coming straight down through his crown chakra to the base of his spine. The ray of sunshine would then fill his whole body and give healing energy to all areas. I then had Rob imagine that he could see an image of himself in a mirror. Given his age, this was easier than superimposing his image on a screen. When he could see the image, I had him imagine that he was being drawn closer to the mirror image by an invisible thread. I asked him to relax further as he was getting closer to his image and to take a deep breath and when he released his breath, he would find himself inside this image in the mirror. I then asked Rob to look around to have a look at the lungs and to see if they were a uniform colour.

Next, I told him to imagine that the front of the lungs were like honeycomb and that all the little hexagonal holes had a door on them. I asked him to watch closely as he took a breath and to notice how the doors opened inward to let air into the lungs and then had him take note of how the doors opened to let the air out and in his case, not as many of the doors opened. I then had him imagine that he had a can of spray that could loosen the hinges on the doors. I suggested he spray each hinge on every door of the honeycomb on both lungs. This took some time, but when he had finished doing so, I asked him to take a deep breath and watch as the hinges opened. While he was exhaling, he could see that the hinged doors let the air out of the lungs. I bought him back to his haven and after a short rest, I had him return to the now. I let him recover from his ordeal as it had taken him half an hour to do this work. I then had him repeat what he had done to fix his problem. It is amazing how a person can recall the tiniest detail while under alpha/theta but can also overlook some major development. This happened with Rob. He could not recall how he got into the mirror image but could explain in detail the honeycomb, the doors and how many hinges would not move. He could also describe spraying each hinge and then watching all the doors swing both ways when inhaling and exhaling.

I then explained to them that this was not a cure for asthma, but a means to enable him to breathe easier. I also reminded him that each time he used his 'puffer' he would be keeping the hinges working with the spray.

It was still 1995 when I received a phone call from Tony who had been given my card by another of my patients. Tony said that he was a paraplegic and asked if he could come and see me one Sunday morning. I confirmed a time and looked forward to meeting him to see if I could help. When Tony arrived with his mother, I was surprised to see that he was driving the car. He took his wheelchair from the back seat of the car, assembled it and then made his way to the lounge room without any assistance before I listened to his story.

Apparently the accident had occurred about two years earlier. Tony had been repairing the corrugated iron roof of his house when he stepped on a loose piece of iron and went over the edge of the roof. It was a three-metre drop to the ground and he landed on his feet with his back bent over his knees. His head had gone to one side and his backside to the other. The fall resulted in three broken vertebrae and he was taken for surgery immediately. During the operation, he had a 25cm steel rod attached to his spine and had not had any feeling from his armpits to the soles of his feet ever since. Tony had a catheter inserted to his bladder as he had no control over that area. Surprisingly enough, he did have control over his bowel movements. We got Tony onto the table and I was able to inspect his back. My first reaction was 'What a mess!'

I felt a hot spot just below the bottom of the rod in his back. I checked this hot spot and as I was massaging the area, I gave a gentle push and heard a click. I knew that a disc had returned to its rightful place. Tony turned and looked at me in wonder. He said that it felt as if his bladder wanted to work. This was the first time in two years that he had felt this sensation and he was amazed. In the bathroom Tony removed his catheter and found that he could stop and start the flow of urine. The return of such a basic body function was a cause for great joy for Tony.

I continued to massage Tony from his shoulders to his waist. As I did so, I felt some more of his discs move back into place. This was the first time that Tony had been massaged. His physiotherapy treatment at the hospital had concentrated on moving his joints, not on massaging his body. In total, Tony's first visit took two hours. When he was preparing to leave, he said that he felt great and that he would be back in two weeks time. Over the next six months Tony continued to visit me and each treatment we did took about two hours. He was noticing improvement after each visit. After six months he had feeling down to his waistline and I knew that the next part of his treatment was going to be the hardest.

For my next treatment session I visited Tony's house. He had a split staircase inside which consisted of seven steps, a small landing and then eight more steps. I watched as Tony wheeled himself to the bottom step. He then took a cushion and placed it on the bottom step, manoeuvred himself out of the chair onto the cushion and tied the tapes that had been sewn onto the edge of the cushion around his waist. He then began to go up the stairs backwards, one step at a time. He would place both hands on the step behind him and then lift his body up to that step. This process was repeated until he was at the top. I watched in amazement and wondered just how much power he exerted to lift the dead weight of his body from step to step. When we were upstairs, I began my treatment. I started the massage and sent healing energy into his waist and buttocks. When he told me that he could feel my hands working in this area, I knew that this part of the body was responding.

That afternoon we went to a small swimming pool. Tony's way of getting into the pool was to aim his wheelchair down the ramp and let go. As soon as he was waist deep he could float out of the chair with ease and could manoeuvre his body into the deeper area. When he was chest deep I watched with excitement as he began to slowly move his legs. The massage from that morning was now working. Muscles that had lain dormant for almost three years were now beginning to work, ever so slowly. After half an hour in the pool, Tony was almost exhausted. He had been moving his legs from the hips the whole time he was in the water, which really was an amazing feat for a paraplegic. When we arrived back at Tony's house I asked him to sit on the bottom step for a moment as I had been thinking about the fact that he had been moving his legs from the hips and had an idea. I asked him to think about the movements that a child makes when it is first beginning to crawl. This thought process would allow him to make those same steps in his quest to become mobile again. I then asked him to turn over and begin to crawl up the stairs. The first two movements were hard. He had to reach behind him and drag his leg on to the bottom step. A short time later he was able to lean to one side to get his leg to the next step. He then leant to the other side and repeated the movement. It took Tony 12 minutes to navigate the 15 steps. That wasn't counting the ten minute break that he took on the landing, which allowed him to get his energy back. When Tony arrived at the top landing he called his mother to come and watch. He slid forward down to the first landing, turned around and came back up. This time the process took just over five minutes and Tony kept saying "This is another obstacle overcome".

Before this time, Tony had been moving around the house by using his wheelchair or by dragging himself along, similar to the way he had demonstrated on the stairs. After this conquest, he found that he could crawl almost anywhere. One problem was that he couldn't feel his knees or his toes, but that was not enough to stop his progress. After three more visits to my place, Tony had feelings right down to about two inches (5cm) above his ankles. Needless to say, he was delighted with this development.

At this point of the treatment, I decided to take the big test. I had Tony stand, with my help, and he leant against the wall. His balance was a bit shaky for a few minutes, which was to be expected. He then started to move sideways, ever so slowly, but he succeeded in moving about ten feet towards the doorway.

Here he put his hands across the open space to the doorjamb and moved to the opposite side with my assistance to hold his hands.

At this time, he complained that the steel rod in his back was holding him back in some movements. He decided it was time to have it removed. The doctors were amazed that a man who was supposed to be paralysed from the armpits down could stand and move around. They decided to remove the plate. Six weeks later, Tony came to see me and was very thankful for everything that we had accomplished. He said "Without you, I would still be a lump of meat sitting in a wheelchair." I have not seen Tony for about four years now, but I receive a Christmas card each year in which he thanks me again for taking the time to give him his life back.

After talking about the previous two healings, it is perhaps pertinent to ask whether I approach such 'major' healings like cancer and paralysis with the same confidence that I do a sore knee or a stiff neck. Obviously, treating cancer or paralysis is much more complex and it does take longer. However, I once again must emphasise that it is my healing spirits who are doing the 'work' and not me. When I am given my message how to treat each patient, I follow the directions with the same desire no matter what the complaint. Treating such things successfully however, does reinforce once again just what a wonderful gift that I have been given. I am still in awe of what I can accomplish with the guidance of my healing spirits. It is something that I ponder all the time and will never take for granted the amazing things that I can do as a healer and I often ask why I was chosen to do this work. It is interesting to reflect on how I became aware of my God given gift. What if I had never studied first aid or met Mr Martinovich? It seems impossible to imagine my life without my role as a healer. I truly believe that if it hadn't been for these factors, then it would have been something else that led me to my ultimate discovery. I don't believe it is a gift that I could have remained totally unaware of, as it is now such an integral part of my life and who I am. I have never been fearful of my great gift, nor have I ever tried to shy away from using it. I know that I am here to serve others and to help them when they are suffering.

CHAPTER NINE
A Growing Reputation

I had a phone call from a woman that I knew who explained that her husband Ashley had a sore back and a stiff neck and could not turn or move. I asked her to send Ashley down to me, but she informed me that he did not believe in Quack or Witchcraft type of medicine and was adamant that he would get no benefit from visiting me. I then asked this woman if she would give permission for me to do an absent healing on her husband. She had never heard of this and so I explained that I would go into deep meditation and imagine that I could see where the problem was. I would then give healing energy to that area and this would fix the problem. I explained that in this case, I would look at the back and do a healing there and not touch the neck. I also said that I would give her a time when I would be finished the healing and then, when her husband came home, I told her to ask him if he had felt anything happen to him at this particular time and to ask him about his back. I said that his reply would let her know whether she should explain what I had done.

Ashley got home for lunch at 12 o'clock and was at my place about 10 minutes later. He wanted to know all about the healing and how it was possible to heal his sore back when I wasn't even present. I explained the whole absent healing process and said that we might as well do something about his sore neck while he was there. I massaged the neck for about two minutes and found what the problem was. I put a little pressure on the spot and massaged for another minute. In that short space of time, the ailment was solved and the pain had gone. Ashley was able to look over his shoulder and to move his neck backwards and forwards again. He wanted to know how I knew where to find and cure the sore spot. I replied "I was guided by my healing spirit".

In 1996, I had an opportunity to experience something completely different. A company had just received a camera that was apparently capable of taking a photo of the aura. I was asked if I would sit for my aura to be photographed. Given that I had been explaining auras and teaching about them on the Sunshine Coast for a number of years, I obliged. I was instructed to sit in a chair and there was a metal pad by my left hand. I had to place my hand on this pad.

When all the equipment was ready, the photograph was taken. It was Polaroid type film that developed within a minute and so I didn't have long to wait until I saw the photo. There was a murmur of amazement as the photo was passed around and studied. For some reason a large aura of deep red covers my head. A distinct circle of gold colour is visible over my head and around the red. There were some other colours visible as well, including blue over my neck, lilac over my heart and yellow over the left lung area. The most striking feature was the gold band, which some people suggested might be a halo. I don't know about that, but it was certainly an amazing feat of technology to be able to show my aura in this way.

Jo came to see me with a back and hip problem and when I massaged her back, I was directed to go to the feet. Sure enough one leg was 25mm shorter than the other. I gave the short leg a gentle flick and pull at the same time. When I measured them again, both legs were the same length. After another two minutes of massage and some pressure on the hot area, a click let me know that the disc had returned to the right place. In less than five minutes, Jo affirmed that she was fine once again and there was no pain in either her hip or back.

Back and neck problems are probably the most common complaint that I treat. I can generally tell what is wrong with somebody by observing them as they walk up the driveway to the house. When they are in obvious pain, it will often affect the way they walk and carry themselves. Once they are lying down on the massage table, it does not take me long to find the source of the complaint. Areas that are hot are the most obvious and it does not take me long to place my hand on somebody's back or neck and detect a hot spot. Even if they have not told me specifically what the problem is, I can almost immediately point out the painful area.

Ingrid came to see me in 1996 claiming that her hip must be broken because it was causing her so much pain. I was a little surprised at this because she had walked into my house without even a limp. She was a very bright and bubbly person who was also very talkative. I had Ingrid lie down on the massage table and then proceeded to seek out the cause of her pain.

A quick look at her feet was enough to indicate that a disc at the base of her spine was out of place. This is a particularly common problem when people present with any kind of back problem and it is very easily fixed. I gave the area a healing massage and then flicked and pulled the leg at the same time. As usual, the disc then resettled back into the normal position. When I told Ingrid that her treatment was complete and that she should be pain free, she got off the table talking all the while. She wriggled her hips, bent over and touched her toes, jumped and stretched. Then she began to talk at a rate of knots. "Ron you had me on the table for about one minute. You pulled my leg and then tell me that I'm better. I feel better and I have no pain. So how do you do it? You hardly even touched me. How can you find what is wrong with me when you didn't even ask?"

With some effort I managed to interrupt her and gave her something to think about. I explained that my healing spirit did the work and as always, I was just the medium that the healing comes through. Ingrid went away happy and with something important to ponder. Ingrid became a regular patient after that visit.

Joan had been to see me a few times since her tumour removal in 1995. We had spoken about her experiences and she was very critical of the medical profession. In her opinion, patients were shuffled from GP to specialist to x-ray to scanners and other equipment and then back to the specialist. She reiterated that being diagnosed with a serious illness is certainly bad enough but this whole process does not help matters at all. She explained that I was now the only person that she would trust to do any healing on her. I took this as quite a compliment, but most of all, I was just happy that my gift had assisted in healing her.

One day in 1997 Joan came limping into my house. Apparently she had kicked an object and as a result, had hurt her foot. All her adult life Joan had been a good ballroom dancer and really enjoyed it as an interest. Joan explained to me that the Queensland Championships were on that night and she and her partner were competing. I began to examine Joan's foot by placing a hand on either side of it and then waited for a message to come through. I then touched the middle of the upper foot and got the expected exclamation of "Ouch!" I began to gently massage and found the broken bone. It was not out of place by much and I was able to manipulate the bones back together. Mentally I was able to see what I was doing. In my mind, I applied a special glue, put the ends of the bone together again and cleaned the edges. I was satisfied that the bones would knit together nicely. I again massaged the outside of the foot, toes, heel, instep and sole and right up to the area above the ankle. Joan didn't complain of any discomfort while I was doing the massage. She even asked if she would be able to dance that evening. I instilled in Joan's mind that her foot would not hurt during her three sections of the dancing competition, although at the end of the evening after the dancing concluded it might begin to cause her pain again.

The next morning Joan was back at my place again. She informed me that her foot had not hurt during the afternoon practice. Furthermore in the evening, she and her partner had won each section of the competition , which gave them the championship. She was absolutely delighted. However, while she was sitting in a chair waiting for the presentations, her foot began to twinge. When they were called to the centre of the dance floor, her foot was so sore that she was limping quite noticeably. After hearing her story, I examined the foot again and did a little massage that removed the pain. I then told her that under no circumstances was she to do any more dancing for at least two weeks. The foot healed well but Joan's partner decided to take on a new and younger partner. Joan was devastated and has not danced competitively since.

Joan's injury is a good opportunity to explain what I can do in terms of broken bones. While I can do a healing as detailed above, it is still necessary for the patient to rest and immobilise the affected limb. In Joan's case, I just bought her a bit of time. I would certainly always encourage the patient to have the broken bone examined by a doctor and set in plaster as the healing time is much faster. Rather than taking a broken arm six weeks to heal, it would generally take about two weeks.

Ingrid arrived on my doorstep once again, this time with a migraine headache. Let me again state that I don't advertise myself as a healer. Every patient that I have helped has come to me on a recommendation from somebody else. I also have people who come back on several occasions, as Ingrid had .

Ingrid sat in the chair that I had placed for her and I began to massage across the shoulders and up the neck. As soon as I found the area where the disc was out of place, I gave it a little pressure. A click told me that the disc was back in place. I then massaged the optic nerves for a few seconds, then the temporal area for a few seconds. After I had done this Ingrid confirmed that there was no longer any pain. Once again a debilitating pain was cured in less than five minutes.

As well as conducting these individual healings over the years, I was also busy with group teachings . Generally I don't have more than five people in a group as I find it more effective with smaller numbers. I am always surprised that people come to me with absolutely no knowledge of psychic healing, although I don't see this as any handicap and I certainly encourage people to learn. To assist them, I prepare notes for each student in the class and when everybody has their copy, I begin a discussion on what each person knows and what they would like to know and learn. I also ask them if they are interested in pursuing a career in psychic healing or whether they would just like to be able to help their family and friends.

The first question most often asked is "How do we know if we are psychic healers?" Other common questions are if I can teach them to find their healing guides or if I can teach them to see an aura. I have been asked these questions countless times and although it may seem repetitious, I find answering questions to be thoroughly enjoyable. I also enjoy giving examples about what to expect from the course. It's a great feeling to know that I can help all these students to find their healing potential.

One of the easiest ways for me to explain psychic healing is to have all the students go into a meditation. Then when I feel that they are ready, I have them move from their haven and go to another area. Here I conduct a deep breathing exercise for a few minutes and then I ask them to imagine that they can see a kitten that has been hurt. I guide them through the examination of the kitten and then when they have found the problem, I give them an opportunity to use any cure at their disposal. When they have returned to the now, I then begin to question them one by one as to what happened in their first meditation.

It is amazing how different the stories can be from this ten minute meditation. Some find the kitten suffering from lack of milk, broken limbs, internal problems, fleas and other complaints. However, as they had been guided to heal, all of these problems were solved and the kitten went off happily.

Coral phoned me and asked if I could go to her home approx. 30km away. When I asked her what the problem was, she informed me that she was sick of life and wanted to end it. That got me activated and I was at her house in less than 20 minutes.

When I arrived, I found Coral happily watering the garden. We went inside and after a glass of cool water we began to discuss the problem. Coral's husband had passed away some years earlier and her children had grown up and gone their own way and she was on her own and very lonely. She owned her own little cottage, but had no ready cash saved up as her nest egg had gone towards her husband's funeral expenses and her son's wedding. Coral only worked two days per week and was finding it difficult to meet basic daily living costs. On top of this, Coral's mother wanted her to sell her house and move interstate to live with her. It was fair to say that Coral was very upset.

We had a quiet discussion and after about an hour, I could see one obvious problem. Her Yin-Yang was completely out of balance and there were more negative than positive thoughts running through Coral's brain. I settled her down and asked her to follow my voice without answering or interjecting. I guided Coral through the balancing of her Yin-Yang and also had her remove all unwanted phobias. This part took some time, as I was quite sure that there were some things in the back of her mind that she wanted to hang onto and not change. After instilling faith and love in her mind, I found that Coral settled down quietly and was very calm when we bought her out of deep meditation. Discussing the experience that Coral had been through gave me the insight of a very lonely woman. I do not like becoming involved in any family issues and today was to be no exception.

During the session, Coral informed me that her son needed finances to extend his house and had apparently almost demanded that Coral sell her house and move in with her mother. This was not a simple thing as her mother lived interstate on the edge of a farming area. The change of lifestyle would be enormous. Coral's current home was on a rise about 300 feet above sea level and it overlooked a little village on the shoreline. It also had a 180 degree panoramic view of the South Pacific Ocean and several beaches. Coral had been facing this dilemma for the past three months and was no closer to finding a solution. If she sold her home, it would make her son and her mother happy as her son would have the financial aid he wanted and her mother would have her company. Yet to make them happy, Coral would have to give up what was certainly an enviable lifestyle in a beautiful position.

It took me another hour to convince Coral that now her Yin-Yang was in balance and she was feeling much calmer, she should wait at least two months before making any decisions. I told her to put all those past thoughts into perspective and to reflect on them in her new state of mind. Coral promised to contact me again in the near future.

Almost four months later Coral contacted me again. She seemed excited, calm, depressed and excited – in that order. When I finally get a word in to speak, Coral went very quiet. I asked some questions to try and find out what her immediate problem was. Coral then began to fill me in on the last four months. She had sold her lovely little house and had purchased a second floor, two bedroom unit that was closer to the beach. Her mother had passed away and the pressure from her son for money was still bothering her. She had lost her job and was now surviving on the pension. Her main problem was that she was once again contemplating suicide. This worried me and so I arranged to go to her place as soon as possible.

I found Coral to be in a very calm and happy mood. After talking to her for a few minutes, I could immediately sense that she was a very lonely woman. She went for walks along the beach every morning where she would pass many different people, but would never speak to anybody. These walks started out as half an hour and had gradually extended to more than two hours. Coral found that the beach was the only thing that could relax her – the flat white sands, the gulls and the rolling surf were her saving grace. Noise from other units, cars racing down the street and radios blaring were the things that drove her to the beach to seek some peace.

I asked Coral to give me her reason for wanting to end her life. Her reply was "If I die, my son will get all my possessions and he will then be happy!" This response led me to believe that her Yin-Yang was out of line once again and I would have to help her to balance it. In the meantime I decided to get to the bottom of her problem which proved to be quite easy. It turned out that her son and his wife were now expecting a baby and naturally they wanted to have everything ready for when the baby was born. This was the news that every parent who has raised their own children wishes for, their first grandchild. I explained to Coral that suicide would not help her in any way. It was relatively easy for me to demonstrate the valuable aspects of her life at that time and to compare them to what she was contemplating. I also pointed out that it was something that she did NOT want.

I found out that Coral was very good with her hands. Sewing, knitting and crocheting were all skills that she possessed and they could be put to great use in preparing for her grandchild. She could make clothes, toys and other associated things and in that way, could contribute enormously. As soon as I pointed this out to her, she brightened up and began planning what she was going to do. A few minutes of time utilised in the right way had made the thought of suicide a distant memory for Coral.

Most of my healing work has involved backs and the nervous system, but after treating Dianne in late 1998, I was reminded that the mind is something that I can also help. Dianne's problem was a little bit unusual. Apparently she loved swimming and was very comfortable in the pool until somebody splashed water on her face. That simple action would produce panic and fright in Dianne and she would begin screaming. When I asked her about washing her face or being under the shower, she said that they were not a problem. I pondered this for a moment and then all of a sudden I was given the answer to take her back to a past life and I would find the problem. I put the idea to Dianne and began to explain the way to guide her to the past life where her problem was. I could sense that she was more than willing to find the answer as to why she could not put her face under the water. I made arrangements for a time when we could have at least an hour of solitude. When Dianne arrived at 8.30 the next morning, she was excited at the thought of discovering what or who she had been prior to this life. I settled her in a comfortable armchair and explained how I would guide her through the meditative state. I told her that her mind would provide the answers when we began the journey to the past. Dianne was a good subject. In two minutes she was deep into meditation and secure in her 'haven'. I began by asking Dianne to follow a path. Down this path, she would see all the natural things like flowers, tree branches overhead and green grass. She followed this path to a natural brick wall where she could see an opening between the bricks. I explained that this was the path to take and instructed her to be calm. I told her that after she entered this passageway, she would find that after each step she took, she would get younger. She would see signs of the years for example 15, then further on would be 10 and then 5. At the end of the passage, she would see a light and would find that she was an adult again and yet she would be in another place and another time. I told Dianne to look around and remember who she was, her age and her sex. I then instructed her to go about her business, to do what she was doing before that life came to an end. I explained that only she could see what had caused that life to end and her new one to begin. I told her to take her time and to stay relaxed and also to try and stay calm. I reminded her that she was being guided by her spirit guide.

Dianne became a little restless at this time and I knew it was now the right moment to have her return to this life. I directed Dianne to return to the area where she stepped into the light. She then had to take the step that would have her leave that life and become an infant. She then had to progress up the passage to the one year mark, to walk carefully to five and then more confidently to ten and then twenty. At this point she would find her way between the bricks and back onto the path as an adult. I directed her to take a deep breath and to realise that she was free. I then had her take her time and move slowly along the path, smelling the flowers, feeling the light breeze and the sunshine as it filtered through the trees. I told Dianne that she would notice a small hut on the side of the path and that she had to go to the open door, knock and then enter the room. Inside, there were three wise men and one of the men would give her a message. I told her to remember the words of the wise man. I then instructed Dianne to go back to her haven where she would receive energy from the sun to give her strength and to help her recover from her journey. Dianne was quiet, her breathing was regular and her posture relaxed. I felt that she had recovered and was ready to return to the now. I told Dianne to take a deep breath and as she exhaled, she would find herself sitting on the lounge chair.

Dianne began to smile, opened her eyes and then words began to tumble from her. She realised that she had not moved and her arms were on the armrest of the chair, her legs on the raised footrest and her body was completely relaxed. Gradually she became aware of the situation and after a deep breath, she began to move and talk. It took me a minute to quieten her down as all her experiences were being jumbled one on top of the other. I asked Dianne to explain her journey in order of her different experiences. This is how she related it to me. "I was in my haven by a pool and under a shady tree. Then I was walking down a path. I came to a wall and saw a passageway. I went down this passage and the feeling was wonderful and I was 20 years old again. The further I walked, the younger I became. I crawled over a step and then I was a woman of about 30 years old. The area that I was in was ancient and the people were wearing very old clothing. It looked like an old English village. I could understand what people were saying. Most of the words were about me. Then I heard someone say "She is a witch". I can't remember what year this was, but the next thing I knew some men grabbed me and tied me to a long pole. I was then lowered into a river – I went right under the water and then they lifted the pole out. I seemed to be watching this from a distance as they put me under the water again. I screamed and the water filled my mouth, but I kept screaming anyway. The next thing I remembered was back in the passage and walking past the five-year mark. I became confident as I passed the ten and fifteen mark. I was then a young woman again and was back on the original path. It felt wonderful to be alive as I walked to a little shack and knocked before going inside. It was very dim in there and I heard a gentle voice tell me "Have faith in all things you do". The next thing I remember, I was sitting in a chair feeling very heavy and not being able to move until I heard your voice telling me to take a deep breath and relax".

I told Dianne that I could explain to her in simple terms why she was afraid to put her head under water. In the old days, in the 13th and 14th century, it was a common practice to put any suspected witch on what was called the 'dunking pole'. A person was lowered into the river for about two minutes and then brought back to the surface. If they were still alive, they would be immersed again for another two minutes. This would happen three times. If that person drowned, then it was concluded that they were not a witch. In this situation, their families would get a pardon. If the person was still alive after the third dunking, then that was considered proof that they were a witch and they would be burned at the stake. The logic behind this process was that witches cannot drown but they cannot survive being burned at the stake. In Dianne's case I explained that she was found not to be a witch, but she had drowned in her past life. I also told her that the message she got from the wise men should always be remembered and those words put into practice in her life.

Two weeks later Dianne phoned me and I could tell that she was very excited. After our session she was now able to dive into the pool without fear. This may seem like a small thing but it had been affecting Dianne's life quite considerably. To finally be free of this phobia was truly liberating for her and as always, I felt privileged to have been able to help her.

I have a steady flow of people coming to see me with back pain and would estimate about 90% of my healing work is in this area. A woman came to see me complaining that her lower back and hip area were extremely sore. Apparently she had been to several doctors, had x-rays and had also had physiotherapy but unfortunately to no avail. She explained that she was living on painkillers and this was certainly not an ideal situation. She was desperate to get some relief as even walking was causing great pain in her legs. I asked her to lie on my massage table face down and upon examining her, I found a very hot area at the base of her spine. I gently massaged this area for a few minutes and then I moved on to her feet. I asked her to relax her knees before I moved her legs up and down from the knees. When I placed her legs on the table and held them together, I found that one leg was 2.5cm shorter than the other. I gave the shortest leg a gentle pull and flick at the same time and this brought the legs back to the same length. I massaged the base of the spine and the hip area for a few more minutes and the hot area had cooled down. I then pushed my thumb into the side of the buttocks and massaged the nerves running down her legs. This improved the feelings in the legs, but she still complained of having pain in front of the hip. I asked her to turn over onto her back and then gently massaged the area along the hipbone and stomach. This brought a groan from her and I asked her to relax while I massaged the lower area of her stomach. Both sides were quite sore and so I used the side of my hand to rub along the pelvic bone for a few minutes and this brought relief very quickly.

After about 15 minutes, the woman was free from pain and couldn't believe it after suffering for so long. When she asked me how I had gotten rid of her pain, I explained that as a medium, I followed the directions that came to me from my healing spirit. I have been using this method of pain relief for nearly 50 years and I still wonder how a gentle rub from my hands can relieve the obvious pain so quickly. I do not hesitate to acknowledge the guiding and healing spirits who send me these healing powers. I always give thanks after each healing that I am the medium and the healing comes through me to the person who is receiving the treatment.

Betty made an appointment to see me and explained that she had sore lumps in her armpits and breasts. I came to the conclusion that her lymph glands were not functioning normally and would most probably need some gentle massage to get them functioning again. When she arrived, I explained what I intended to do but she seemed hesitant until my wife confirmed that I had helped many women with the same complaint. Betty had no idea of how the lymph glands functioned in the breast and so I did my best to explain their function and their position in the breast. I found that Betty, like many women, was more shy than ignorant of this problem. To help combat her shyness, I asked her to take three deep breaths to calm her nerves. I gently began working down from the shoulder to the armpit removing the soreness as I worked. I soon discovered a hard lump in the right breast. I moved her hand over this area and had Betty feel the size. When she squeezed the area, the pain became much worse. I began to gently massage this area and moved sideways, then up and down the breast. I did this until I felt that the lymph had opened and had emptied into the gland above, thus allowing the cleaning process to take place. I continued to massage the area for a few minutes more. Betty noted that the lump appeared to have moved and also that the soreness had gone from the area.

I then moved onto the left breast and found only one area by the nipple that was sore. We soon had the lymph glands working on this side and after the session had finished, Betty confirmed that there was no longer any soreness at all.

In one of my many meditations, I experienced something that was very strange. This same event happened three nights in a row, the only exception being that it was a different place each time.

If I ever wake during the night, I have developed a habit of lying quietly and meditating. One particular night I awoke and noted that the time was 2.25am. While meditating, I found myself going into the children's ward of a hospital. Upon entering the ward I noticed that it was overcrowded and there were children on stretchers, in wheelchairs and on beds down the corridors. As I walked down this corridor I placed my hand on each child as I passed. This was only for an instant because I kept walking during that time. When I reached the end of the ward and I had touched the last child, I turned around to retrace my steps. The sight that confronted me left me truly amazed. I looked down the length of the corridor, at each bed and chair and there were no children there. I looked for a nurse or a doctor but there were none to be seen. I looked in and under the beds but the children had just disappeared. Then for no reason at all a quote from the Bible came to me out loud "Suffer the little children to come unto me". I had not read the Bible for a very long time, but I had to wonder if Jesus had used me as his medium to heal these children?

The enormity of the question hit me. I roused from my meditation in quite a state. My heart was pumping rapidly and dozens of questions came to mind. I wondered exactly what had happened and how I had gotten into this situation. Had these children whom I had touched really been cured and sent home? I managed to calm my heartbeat and then lay in my bed and began to recount the event that had happened. The time was now 2.40am – the meditation had lasted 15 minutes.

The following night I did not sleep before meditating. I noted that the time was 11.15pm. In this mediation, I was directed to another hospital. The ward was different and all the children had plaster casts on different parts of their limbs. I walked down the ward touching each child as I passed. When I got to the end of the ward I was again amazed when I turned around to find all the beds empty. The plaster casts were all scattered on the floor and there was not a child in sight. I came out of the meditative state and found that I had been under meditation for ten minutes as the time was 11.25pm. I was quite perplexed. I had not been advised by my healing guide or healing spirit that these events would take place. I accepted that there would be a logical answer. I then slept until about 4.30am without dreaming and woke completely relaxed.

On the third night the same thing happened again. The only difference this time was that I noticed a tingling down the left side of my scalp to the neck. I then remembered that the same thing had happened on each of the other occasions. The mystery was now becoming clearer. When I first began meditating many years ago, I used to get the same feeling of a tingling sensation on the left side of my head when my spirit guide contacted me. Now that I had given some thought to the events of these nights, I am sure that I have been guided in each of these meditations and the healing had been done by them through me as the medium.

I suppose it is fair to say that I have become somewhat accustomed to events such as this happening to me, however, I do not necessarily know what they mean at the time. Often after further meditation I can understand more clearly, but other times I am still mystified. It can certainly be a very unusual experience to have something happen that others would probably find hard to believe. Once again I stress that I am at a loss to understand why I was chosen to do this work and I know that sometimes I just have to accept what happens, without necessarily knowing exactly why.

I would estimate that over the years, I have performed thousands of healings. On average I would treat two people each day, but of course this has varied greatly. On some days I may see ten people and on others, none at all. However, I would have to describe the flow of people to my door, wherever that door may have been, as constant. I have spoken about only a handful of the cases that I have seen and as mentioned throughout this book, backs and necks have been my highest case load. Many of these cases were almost identical, as was their treatment. In almost all cases the problem was fixed in minutes and the patient could walk away pain free. Believe me, there is nothing more rewarding than witnessing that kind of transformation. I have just used a representative sample to demonstrate how common back and neck complaints are and just how simply I (as a medium) can treat them. I could have documented every single one, but that would have taken several books and really the only thing that would be different would have been the names. This doesn't mean that I didn't put the same effort into treating each one or that I viewed such cases as 'just routine'. Rather, I believe that it demonstrates that I have helped a lot of people with a very common complaint. To see the pain some people are in when they arrive, I can appreciate just how much of a difference it must make to their lives to be pain free again.

It is always humbling to have people tell me that I am the 'best' psychic healer they have encountered. I can't answer that, but what I can do is tell them that my healing guides are doing the work and it is certainly a great privilege to have their healing energy flow through my hands. I will always be amazed at how word of mouth can spread news, I have never erected any kind of sign or advertised in the Yellow pages but I have still treated thousands of people. It is very complimentary that these people not only come back themselves on several occasions, but also recommend me to others as well. For reasons that I am unable to fathom, I was chosen to do this great work and I have always done my best to use this gift fully.

Skeptics would say that there is no cure for cancer and in medical terms, there isn't. However I know what I have treated and these people have defied all medical odds and probably stumped their doctors too. In these cases, I have simply followed the advice of my spirit guides and they have done the work through me. The fact that these patients are still alive and well, is the only proof I need that my healing spirits can do things that we don't understand. I accept that there are many things about my work that I don't understand and probably never will, however I will certainly never stop striving to seek knowledge. Nor do I question the things that come to me as psychic messages as they always prove to be exactly right.

When I think back to my first healing experience, it is hard to believe what has unfolded in my life since that time. I cannot imagine my life without this role as a psychic healer. I have never taken it for granted and have always done things to the very best of my ability. I am so very happy to have been able to help so many people and will always remain thankful for my precious gift.

CHAPTER TEN

Your Personal Power System

In this section I will explain some of the more common elements of psychic healing. As I have become more experienced over the years, I have learned a lot on this subject and have come to recognise their valuable role in total physical wellbeing.

The Chakras

The energy from the spiritual, mental and etheric planes, which are used in healing, enters the physical plane through energy centres called chakras. The energy from the higher planes directly affects our emotions and also our physical health. Each of us have seven major chakras (the word chakra in Sanskrit means wheel). They look like long thin funnels with the large opening on the surface of the etheric body. They resemble the old hearing devices used in the nineteenth century.

These chakras act as terminals through which energy or prana is transferred from the higher planes to the physical body. It is essential to know and understand their function to understand their use in healing. In the same way that problems occur in modern rail and air terminals when traffic becomes clogged, problems may occur when energy becomes clogged as it is transferred through the chakras. These problems, which originate on the higher planes, weaken the subtle energy system. The weakness is then transmuted to the physical plane and it creates fertile ground for the development of physical disease. Here is a brief explanation of each of the chakras and their different functions.

First Chakra: Bright red and called the root chakra: Base of the spine or the reproductive area.. It is the channel for subtle energy entering the earth plane, bringing with it vitality which circulates through the body by way of the bloodstream.

Second Chakra:	Bright orange and called the selenic center. It improves mental faculties, creating unblocking with regards to anxiety, resentment and confusion. It can sharpen the mind making you more alert.
Third Chakra:	Brilliant yellow and called the solar plexus or navel center. Our emotional energy flows through this center giving a growing sense of aspiration and quickening our intuition and mood sensitivity. It is the basis of our personality that creates our magnetism to society.
Fourth Chakra:	Very pale to deep green and called the heart center, or love center. Pale green creates new growth to richer greens of love and giving. Dark green is the harvest and prosperity of life through love. We use this chakra to direct positive rays of energy when healing. We must learn to think from the heart chakra to project our consciousness outward from this area.
Fifth Chakra:	Electric Blue and called the throat center. It is the core of human expression and it transmits the intent of the soul. It also transmits healing, creative power and is a major center for mind, body and affairs.
Sixth Chakra:	Indigo and called brow center or third eye. Used for opening up your complete receptivity to the higher psychic realms, it is of paramount importance in absentee healing. The third eye is responsive and receptive to all higher energies in the communicative realms with guides and the spiritual world and with your higher self (sanctuary). By using the heart chakra with the third eye to combine for healing, the energy is increased as the two areas come together with divine love.

Seventh Chakra: It's colour is violet and is called the crown chakra. It opens the vortex of receptivity and corresponds to the highest level of spiritual perfection. The crown chakra can generate energy both inwards and outwards. It can assist the other chakras in balancing the body and can open and direct energy to anywhere throughout the Universe.

The clairvoyant will often see or feel disease in the etheric plane before it manifests in the physical body. It can be seen clairvoyantly using psychic ability and can be felt it with the hands, or seen in the patient's aura. The process of opening and balancing the chakras has a dual purpose.

Firstly, it is necessary to keep your chakras open and balanced to maintain your own good health and positive energy. If a person does have medical problems, bringing the chakras into balance will promote rapid healing and recovery.

Secondly, healing others requires the transfer of positive energy in large amounts to be transferred through the chakras and so they have to be open and well balanced.

A Chakra Meditation

Begin by finding yourself a quiet spot, either sitting upright in a chair or lying down on a bed or floor and the back has to be kept as straight as possible. This meditation to balance the chakras should take about five minutes.

Close your eyes and relax, let your mind wander and don't try to control it. Take deep breaths and count backwards from 5 to 1, visualizing the number in your mind's eye as you inhale. Once relaxed, visualize the divine white light filling your mind. Direct this white light down to the base of your spine, which is the home of your first chakra. As it flows through your body to the base of your spine, feel it cleansing your whole body in a perfect positive manner. Continue breathing calmly so that you're breathing in and out at the same strength. Once you have focused the pure energy or light on the base of the spine, you will experience a tingling sensation in the exact area where the first chakra exists. Change the white light to a brilliant red glow and feel the warm tingling increase. You will feel the area expand, sending a flow outside the body into your aura. As you breathe, feel the red glow sending a shaft of light up to the spleen area, which is the second chakra of the body. As it enters the splenic area, the colour changes to a magnificent orange glow. Breathe in and out of this region a calming, feeling, warmth and a tingling sensation, which positions the exact area of your second chakra.

As you breathe, you will feel the energy expanding, the orange glow increasing in size and sending warmth and colour out of your aura and forming a ring of light around that area. Visualize a shift of light moving across as an orange glow to the solar plexus area and as this is happening, you will notice a tingling sensation moving within your body. As the orange glow enters the third chakra, it changes to a brilliant yellow shade. Continue breathing in a calm manner and visualize the yellow glow expanding and feel the warmth and tingling and expansion. The energy, as it expands, will come to the surface of the body and move out into the aura forming a band of brilliant yellow in the solar plexus region. Now visualize a shift of yellow light moving up to the heart chakra, which is the fourth chakra. As it enters the heart region the yellow shaft of light turns to a soft lime green colour. You will notice this lime green colour begin to expand in and around the heart area, as it does so the warmth increases and the tingling sensation expands throughout this region. You will notice too that the glowing area and tingling sensation is located just above the heart area. As the colour, warmth and tingling expand, you will see the colour move out into the aura and form a ring or band of green light around the body. Visualize a shaft of green light being channelled up to the throat area. As it reaches the throat, visualize the colour changing to an electric blue. At this moment, you will instantly feel a tingling sensation in the region of the fifth chakra. Expand the electric blue and feel the increase in the warmth and tingling. As it expands the colour moves out of the body and forms a bank of blue light around the body in the aura region. You will experience a totally calm feeling once this stage is complete because you are now tuning into the clairvoyant and psychic area.

Visualize a shaft of blue light moving from the throat chakra up to the brow or third-eye region and as you do so, the shaft of light changes to an indigo colour and you will feel a tingling sensation around the third-eye region. This is the sixth chakra. Expand the colour and as you do so, the tingling increases with the warmth. Visualize the colour expanding out of the body and forming a band around the body connecting up with the aura.

Direct a shaft of indigo light up to the crown of the head and as you do so, the colour changes to a brilliant violet, tingles begin and you are drawn to the area where the seventh chakra (or crown chakra) is located. Once there, expand the colour and in turn the tingling sensation and warmth will increase. You should also notice a lightheaded feeling. Visualize the violet colour moving outwards beyond the body to form a band of light around the body and blending into the aura. Once this is achieved, feel the overall tingles blending together in harmony and the whole body generating at the same rate. The chakras are now balanced and in tune and so is your aura. You are now with one, with the All. Once tuned, affirm "I am in harmony and in balance with my creator in a positive manner. All is well in my world."

Count backwards from 5 to 1 and as you reach 3, say to yourself, "I am back to the now" and on reaching 1, open your eyes and feel a new energy entering your life. Both the mind and the breath are your main tools at your service for balancing the chakras. The technique of chakra balancing only takes three to four minutes, but even in such a short time, the results can be remarkable. Not only are they open, but balanced, creating a healthy integration of energies that in turn strengthen and revitalize the physical body's energy system. The subtle energy system is strengthened also and this safeguards you from negative encounters from both your internal and external environment. Many people compare its effects to meditating for half an hour or more.

When stuck for time, this is a good alternative. It should ideally be practiced twice a day, morning and night, but not before retiring at night because it tends to stimulate the nerves and keeps you awake.

By practicing regularly, you will find your mind becoming more alert, yet more calm and able to cope with every day chores with an element of joy. You will also experience channels opening more freely with your healing. Your energy levels will increase, filling you with a greater sense of well being. The practice stimulates the flow of prana into the physical body, allowing the body to heal and renew itself more quickly. By healing yourself, you will become more effective in healing others.

I have used the chakras in healing on several occasions. One day I was able to get to the affected area by sending a colour from my chakra to the chakra of a patient. For instance, sending a red colour from the base of the spine to the same area of the patient would assist in healing that area. Green from the heart to the heart would also give relief to any pain in that area. Let me now explain. When I say to see a red colour, this is done by concentrating on the colour and then on the area of the patient's problem and allowing the colour to flow to that area. The patient must be receptive to allow the healing to take place. Also I learned that chakra balancing had a very calming effect on a patient or on any person who would like to have their chakras balanced.

At a circle one night, we used some chakra therapy by seating people in a circle. I began the session by asking them to begin a meditation and when I felt that they were all calm, I began to guide them into accepting the colours. Firstly, I asked them to imagine a shaft of light penetrating through their crown chakra to the base of the spine. When they had the light at the spine, they were then to imagine the colour turning red and to allow the red to be absorbed by the area of the root chakra. When the area was filled they would allow the second chakra to turn the colour to a bright orange. When the area was filled with the orange they had to imagine the shaft of light now moving to the third chakra, and becoming a brilliant yellow. This yellow would fill the third chakra area before moving to the fourth chakra, the heart center, where the colour would turn to a pale deep green. They had to allow this green colour to fill the heart chakra area completely before moving to the throat area, the fifth chakra. In turn, they had to allow this area to be completely filled with pale blue and then watch as the sixth chakra, the third eye area, turn a beautiful indigo colour. This would fill the third eye area then proceed to the crown chakra where the lovely violet/purple would fill the crown chakra. When this area was filled, they had to sit back and relax for around 10 minutes to allow the tranquillity to empower them. This method of healing is very handy when a patient needs calming prior to a healing.

Chakras are very useful in helping people to relax. One day I had the members of the circle sit on the floor with their legs outstretched in front of them and asked them to imagine that a bright red colour was coming into their feet from the toes. I told them to watch as the red crept up the legs to the knees and then higher to the hips. The red would then fill the body to the waist and continue on to fill the chest and then further to the neck now being filled and then the head. "Now I want you to imagine that your crown chakra is now open."

"Focus again on your toes, and imagine an Indigo blue coming through your toes and beginning to fill your legs. As the blue begins to rise, you will notice that it will push the red upwards and as this happens, the red will begin to go out through the crown chakra into the atmosphere. The blue will fill the body to the waist, then to the chest, as more red goes into the atmosphere. The blue will continue to fill the body, the arms and the head. All the red is now gone. Concentrate on your toes again and you will notice a beautiful green filtering through your toes into your legs. As this happens, you will notice that the blue is moving upwards as the green begins to fill the body. The blue is disappearing through the Crown Chakra as the green fills the waist, the chest, the arms and then the head. The blue is all gone and the body is full of emerald green."

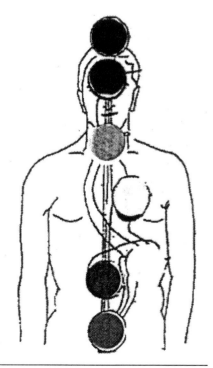

"Now imagine an amber colour seeping through your toes and this will travel faster as it is a light colour. The amber is now moving to your waist and chest, while the arms will fill as the green moves out of the crown chakra. Now the amber will fill the whole of the body.

Next, I want you to imagine that a canary yellow is coming in through your toes and this colour will also move quickly as it is a light pastel colour. Imagine now that the yellow is moving up the leg and the amber is going from the crown chakra. The yellow moves to the waist, the chest, the arms and the head. The amber is all gone and the yellow is now filling the body. Now pay attention to your toes again. I want you to imagine all the pure white that you possibly can. This white will now begin to fill your legs, the hips, the waist, and will then move to the chest. The yellow is moving out of the body and the pure white now fills the rest of your body. I then want you to close your crown chakra, and keep the white in the body. The white represents Peace and Harmony and will allow you to relax in comfort".

THE AURA

Most people have heard the term, Aura. Being able to see your own aura or that of another person can take practice and awareness, but it is certainly a wonderful thing to be able to do. Here is a basic explanation about auras and their role.

The three auras are:

The spiritual aura
The mental aura
The etheric aura

Each one is linked with prana, the spiritual aura having the highest frequencies. The spiritual aura extends the farthest from the body. It has a radius of about twenty five feet in a healthy human being. Within it, is the mental aura, which is composed of energy from the mental body. This extends about eight feet in a healthy human being and reflects the mental state of the person. The final aura reflects the emotional and physical health of the person. This is called the etheric aura and it extends about eight inches from the physical body.

In healing, we are primarily concerned with the etheric aura because when disease is present in either the etheric or physical body, it disrupts the normal flow of energy in the healthy frequencies and changes it, in form, into unhealthy ones. With a shift in frequency, there is also a shift in colour in the etheric aura of the patient. The healer can see when the normal colours, indicating good health, become muddy, dirty or change from bright clear primary colours to earth tones. Browns, greys and black are all associated with disease.

By examining the colours and qualities of the patient's aura, a healer can tell the nature and severity of the patient's disease and can determine the kind of energy the patient needs to regain their health and balance. Then the healer can project the necessary healing energy, in the appropriate colour to their patient. There are three ways the healer can see a patient's aura.

1) By developing his auric vision.

2) By feeling the auras through the palms of his hands.

3) By seeing the aura clairvoyantly.

Seeing the Aura

Four basic conditions must be met in order to physically see the etheric aura. Firstly, the observer must be in alpha/theta level. Secondly, the heart chakra must be open. Thirdly, the room must be darkened and a dark background must be behind the person being viewed. Finally, the observer must allow his eyes to unfocus without straining them.

The aura is mostly readily seen around the head, hands and feet. You should begin looking for the aura around your hands. To see the aura around your hands, you will need a black piece of cardboard about three feet long and eighteen inches wide. To begin, sit upright with your back straight and start breathing yogically. Continue with the yogic breath for two or three minutes and then begin a short meditation. At first, meditate for at least ten minutes using the techniques you've already learnt. This will bring you firmly into the alpha/theta state, and you will be thinking in pictures rather than words. I suggest that after you have counted backwards from 5 to1 or 10 to1 and after you have relaxed your body completely, you must go to your sanctuary and remain there for five minutes. When you return from there, mentally affirm "I am perfectly relaxed, feeling better than I did before and able to see the aura." Then count down from 5 to 1 and when you open your eyes, look down past your hands and into the cardboard below them. For best results, your hand should be held three inches above the cardboard in a horizontal position, palms up with the fingers pointing towards each other and almost touching. The fingers should be comfortably spread out. Once you've begun looking past your hands and through your fingers, your eyes will unfocus without any difficulty. Bring your attention to the heart chakra and begin breathing from it and you will see the aura appear between your fingers.

At first, the aura may be faint and difficult to see and it might look like steam evaporating, but if you continue to relax, going deeper and paying attention without concentrating, the aura will get better. As the brightness grows stronger, colours will begin to emerge. When this happens, slowly spread your hands apart and you will see lines of force connecting your fingers. These lines will connect the corresponding fingers of each and will join them together until you have spread the hands six or eight inches apart. The lines will then split down the middle and the aura will flow around the hands separately. After you have mastered this technique, it will become progressively easier for you to see colours around your friends and associates. The aura around their heads will be the easiest for you to see. You need only observe them while you are relaxed in the alpha/theta state with your heart chakra open and when they have a clear darkened background behind them.

When you want to see another person's aura, use one of the methods you learned earlier to put yourself into the alpha/theta state, unfocus your eyes and look past them into a clear background. The aura around the head will emerge as a mist, then in colours with the darkest colours emerging first, followed by lighter ones. The aura will resemble the halos that you have seen in portraits of saints. Once you've mastered the technique, the auric colours will become bright or even brighter than the colours you see in the material world.

The Auric Colours

Following is a list of major colours found in the human aura and what they indicate concerning emotions and physical health. This is an initial guide only and as you progress you will make your own list based on your own observations.

You should note that within the etheric aura, there is sometimes a narrow band of uniform colour surrounding the physical body. It usually looks dark or colourless and often appears as a gap between the physical body and the etheric aura. It is not seen around everyone, but for those who have it, it doesn't appear to affect them in a negative way. It is an interesting anomaly, which for convenience sake is called the physical aura.

RED GROUP

These have the lowest visible vibration. They have a dual nature in the positive form when bright and clear and their aspects are energising, warming and exciting. The negative aspect ranges from rebellion, contentious, anger, malice, destruction and hate. Dark red indicates selfishness and lack of nobility. Deep red indicates passion. Muddy red indicates the passions becoming unclear and unwholesome. Red with brown in it indicates fear and when the brown darkens and becomes black, it indicates malice. Red with a tinge of yellow indicates uncontrolled emotions and desires. A light red indicates a nervous temperament and bright clear red shows vitality, generosity and material health. A rosy brightness shows family affection and love of the home, while red that moves into pink shows happiness and tenderness.

ORANGE GROUP

In it's clearest form this indicates forcefulness and vitality. When it becomes reddish, it tends to indicate self-centredness.

YELLOW GROUP

This is the colour of intellect. If dull, it indicates a mundane intellect nature. When brighter and moving into gold, it indicates elevation of the intellect and becomes purified through spirit. Muddy or dirty yellow indicates cunning, greed and self-centred egotism.

GREEN GROUP

The colour of balance/colour of the heart. Emerald green, which is clear and bright, is the colour of healing. A great deal of emerald green in a person's aura indicates an interest of involvement in the healing arts. Green is the central colour in the spectrum of light. Balance is harmony and flexibility. Light green indicates harmony, peacefulness and an affinity to nature and the outdoors. In it's negative form, it indicates extreme selfishness. Muddy or dirty in colour, it shows deceitfulness and greed. Brownish green indicates jealousy.

BLUE GROUP

Blue relates to religious feelings and intuitive understanding. Just as green is associated with healing and the heart, blue in it's highest form is associated with the third eye, inspiration and the higher forms of intellect. It is one of the first colours a healer sees. When the blue deepens into an indigo, we find a person with a devotional character and deeply religious spirit. On the negative side, blue with brown or black indicates perversion of religious feelings and fascination with the darker side of spirituality.

VIOLET GROUP

Being a combination of red and blue, it points to even loftier spiritual ideals and power. Those who have violet in their aura are very advanced in their spiritual evaluation. It is the colour of royalty and indicates nobility of character and acts as an insulator and purifier. It comes from the highest realms and thus, is seen only in spiritual masters and adepts. Lavender indicates high spirituality as well as vitality. Lilac shows compassion and living for the good of others. Violet first appears above the head and appears similar to an egg shape on top of the crown chakra. As the expert advances, the violet radiates from there, filling the entire aura with it's light.

BROWN GROUP

A colour made up of other colours. Made up in the negative, even though indicated by many as a business and industry colour, it is the colour most often associated with physical disease. Most healers associate brown with negative human characteristics. In its various forms, it indicates meanness, green and the lower material instincts. Only when it becomes a golden brown does it's vibration rise, showing an industrious, organized character and a methodical temperament.

BLACK GROUP

Absence of light, indicates darkness on all levels. The exception is when it appears in a narrow band between the physical body and the etheric aura and what we call the physical aura.

GREY GROUP

Another negative colour, showing a dull, conventional character that shows a lack of vitality and which is often associated with disease. Heavy deep greys indicate fear, confusion and often dull, heavy, leaden personality often bordering on morbidity. Grey in the aura often indicates an unreliable, deceptive character.

WHITE GROUP

This is the synthesis of all colours which indicates complete integration and the capacity for union. It is the colour of Christ Consciousness, of the I AM, the colour of spiritual perfection and is found only in those who have achieved union and who have attained enlightenment.

Feeling the Aura

Each of us have the capacity to feel the etheric aura, as well as see it. Feeling the surface of the etheric aura is a common method of psychic diagnosis. The healer, by stroking the surface of his patient's aura with the palms of his hands, can collect information about the physical health and emotional wellbeing of his patient. Stroking the surface of the etheric aura is a simple technique.

Have your patient lie on their back and totally relaxed. Use the yogic breathing exercise for a few moments to tune into the etheric aura. Since changes can occur in your patient's aura as a result of strong feelings, excitement or anxiety, having your patient relaxed is essential for receiving accurate impressions. Put yourself into your alpha/theta state. Once there, affirm "I am now in the alpha/theta level and my hands are becoming sensitive." Pass the hands completely over your subject's body three times, starting at the head and ending at the feet.

These passes should be made with both hands about eight inches above the patient, palms down, with fingers loosely extended. Hands should not be touching. After completion, have your patient close his eyes and place your more sensitive hand about eighteen inches above his heart. Let your hand descend until you feel a slight resistance. This may make the palm of your hand tingle. The resistance comes from the surface of your patient's aura. As you know, the etheric aura extends about eight inches from the physical body and although it is fluid and porous throughout, it does have a skin-like surface.

Only then will you receive accurate impressions of the aura's strength and texture.

If you allow your hands to pass through the surface, you will feel the energy of your own hand as it is reflected form your patient's body. If  you get close enough to his physical body, you will feel the heat generated by his body and nothing more. Skim the entire body and notice the sensations in your palm. Become aware of any changes in the aura's energy level that causes your hand to dip towards your patient's body or be pushed further away from it. Sharp changes signify problems in your patient's auric field and subtle energy system. Note differences in temperature as cold spots and warm spots can indicate the presence of disease.

The aura should be firm, smooth and of a uniform temperature. Whenever this varies, this normally indicates disease. After you have registered all the impressions from the front of your patient's body, have them turn over or imagine to turn them over, reverse your hands and again go over the body three times.

It might help to keep a note book and catalogue your findings. Each disease gives off a specific vibration and if you work intuitively, you will learn to discern the subtle distinction of different diseases.

Seeing the Aura Clairvoyantly

To see the aura clairvoyantly, begin breathing yogically and then use the technique you learned earlier to enter the alpha/theta level. After your return from your sanctuary, mentally affirm "I am now in the alpha/theta level and feeling better than I did before." Visualize a screen six feet in front of you, mentally repeat your patient's name and that patient will appear on the screen. Begin scanning your patient's body paying attention to anything that doesn't look right. Problems, if any, will stand out and will be drawn to your attention.

You might be looking at the aura the hand and suddenly you'll be drawn to the knee. When that happens, you can be sure there is a problem with the knee. Look at the colour, texture and strength of it. Go inside the physical body and look for any physical manifestation of disease. Find out if the disease in the aura has been transported to the physical body. In major diseases like cancer or heart disease you will probably see negative colours in the aura. You might not see the connection between various problems in the aura and the physical manifestation, but if this happens, you must follow up by projecting your consciousness inside your patient's physical body. As an example, in heart disease you would see muddy colours in the aura above your patient's chest, but until you go inside the patient you won't know the exact nature of the disease and your diagnosis will be incomplete. If your diagnosis is incomplete, then your treatment may also be incomplete.

Clairsentience and Diagnosis

Not only can you see disease in your patient's aura, but also you can feel their disease. The ability to do this is called clairsentience. Most psychics and healers have it and it is important for healers to develop this because it shows intunement nature, which is essential for healing. Your body is an instrument that can register discomforts from another person's body when you attune yourself to this vibration. At all times, expect to feel unusual sensations in your own body when you do a diagnosis.

Your subtle energy system will be receiving data from your patient and it will register the information as feelings, sensations and minor discomforts. These discomforts are temporary and will have no lasting effect. It is a form of psychic communication, which you should pay attention to and learn to use in diagnosis. The aura, as you see it, is visible clairvoyantly. It can be felt with the palm, can be seen physically and can be felt clairsentiently. Diagnosing from the aura should be part of your psychic diagnosis. As you scan your patient's body, always look at his aura and use this auric vision along with your clairvoyance and clairsentience. They go hand in hand and most healers I know use these methods in combination for psychic diagnosis.

Crystal Dowsing
The art of dowsing goes back a long way and it is something that I have had some success with. On one occasion I did a session with a group using this particular method. I began by giving each of the group a quartz crystal,

approx. 3.5cm long, to which I had attached a leather thong. I then proceeded to show them how to get the crystal to work for them. Holding the thong and allowing the crystal to hang to within 2.5cm from the tabletop was the first step and then, after placing the hand holding the thong against the forehead, they had to wait for the crystal to stop moving. The next step was to have them ask the crystal to give them a positive movement. This could cause the crystal to move in one of three ways.

Some had the crystal rotate clockwise,
some had the crystal rotate anti-clockwise
and others had it swinging sideways.

When each was sure they knew which was the positive, I then had them ask the crystal for the negative. This is usually the opposite to the positive. When all were sure that they could follow the movements and remember them, I had them ask a question of the crystal. I did not tell them that we couldn't ask a question about the future, nor did I tell them that a question that could have two answers would not be answered. The joy of the moment was broken when one lady said that her crystal did not work. I asked what question she had put to her crystal. Her reply was "Crystal, will I have good luck or bad luck?" I then explained to the group that, as this type of question could have two answers, the crystal will only answer one question at a time. You have to ask your crystal one question at a time and then get your answers.

I also told them that questions about the future would get a doubtful response, although on one occasion, I asked about a future event and was told that as the future had not happened yet, there could be no answer.

Clairvoyants have made calculated guesses about future events such as relationships, financial conditions, moving home and health among other things. I am not in any way trying to influence anyone as to the ability of any mortal to either predict or not to predict the future.

About the Author

Ron Wilding is a humble man who has enriched and helped many people from all parts of the world. He always hastens to assure all his patients that he is only a channel for people to experience the healing power of the Great Spiritual Force that is with us all.

Going through a Near Death Experience has had an enormous effect on Ron Wilding and he says that he will never forget the feeling of peace, tranquillity and freedom from all pain and suffering. This has helped him to further appreciate and understand the power of Spirit in our lives and the importance of being in harmony with nature.

He has travelled and worked in many parts of the world including England, Papua New Guinea, New Zealand, Europe and America and now lives on the Sunshine Coast in South East Queensland. Ron still does healing and massage and also uses other therapies as part of his ongoing vocation. He devotes time to Sports Therapies on a regular basis. His reputation ensures that his services will be sought after for many, many years to come.

Ron Wilding regards the time when Johnny Two Birds, a distinguished healer in America, came to his room for a massage and clearing, as one of the most memorable moments of his life. This was the first time that anyone had done a healing on Johnny.

Ron devotes lot of his time to teaching and helping others to use their own skills effectively and he looks forward to many more years as a medium for Healing Spirit.

He loves people and life and is thrilled when the young girl from next door (10 months old) comes to stay for the day with him and his wife, Gloria.

This is Ron's first book and he dedicates it to his lovely wife, Gloria, and to the many wonderful human beings who have enriched his journey.

Testimonials

Ron has helped people with physical and mental problems. The Lord has blessed Ron with the ability to heal others and make a difference in their lives.

Theresa Jowett ...Australia

When I first saw Mr. Wilding I was apprehensive about him touching my neck to relieve a migraine headache but within two minutes of treatment, all pain had gone. I have not had a recurrence of migraine for the last 10 years

Laura Comer ...Seattle Washington USA.

Having had a job for many years that involved heavy lifting, the resultant neck and back pains experienced have been eased since Ron has treated me. No other practitioner has helped to the same degree. His ongoing advise on many everyday ailments has been most helpful to my family and myself.

Amanda Hill ...Australia

Ron worked on my sore back for less than 3 minutes and all the pain was gone.

Peter McKay ...Australia

My husband took me to see Ron as he had a reputation to relieve pain with his therapies. I had severe Migraine and after only one visit, I was relieved of pain.

A year later, I went to see Ron regarding a back problem and after 3 or 4 minutes treatment the pain had gone. To this day, some 8 years later, I have not had this pain again.

Shirley Anson - Smith ...Australia

I first met Ron Wilding about seven years ago through word of mouth, when I was at a stage in my life where I was looking for some direction and deeper purpose. I called Ron and he told me he was running a course on spiritual healing and I knew from the moment I spoke to him that he was the teacher I had been looking for. Ron took me under his wing, along with his wife Gloria and they became like surrogate parents to me.

Ron taught me everything he knew and then asked me if I would like to be his offsider and help him teach other students. The day I met Ron changed my life forever and I will be eternally grateful. Ron has helped me to be the person I want to be and has given me the tools so that I can help my family, friends and anyone else that needs my help, through spiritual healing.

I remember not long after the Ron's course, I was on holidays at Moreton Island, when a Japanese tourist stood on a sting ray and was in immense pain and could not walk on her foot. I gave her a hands on healing and about 15 minutes later, she got up and started jumping up and down with excitement and disbelief that her pain was gone and her foot was as good as new.

Another experience was when I found out my sister had a brain tumor, that was about six years ago, I did an absent healing on her not long after, as she lives in the United Kingdon and I was in Australia. Helen is still alive and well today.

I could go on and on, but there is one other healing that was very inspiring. A lady called Ron one day in desperation as her 25 year old daughter had been diagnosed with a brain tumor, or should I say brain tumors and was told she had 3-6 months to live. Amanda and her mother had tried everything and were willing to give anything a try. Ron, myself and the six or so students participating in the spiritual healing course, were given a photo of Amanda and her permission for us to do a healing on her. So we all did an absent healing on her as a group. Not long after, Amanda went back to the doctor to get more tests done, and when the tests came back, the tumors had all disappeared. That was all the confirmation Amanda need to know she was cured. That was about five or six years ago and Amanda is still alive and well today.

Some people say "oh, it's just a coincidence". I think if you have faith you can be healed, you can be. At the end of the day, when people can be cured of pain and disease in the body, including so called incurable diseases, it doesn't matter how it happens the main thing is, IT HAPPENS! The beauty is that anyone can be a healer, all you need is the tools to be shown how. Ron Wilding can teach you just that.

With nearly sixty years of gained knowledge and experience in the art of healing, Ron has so much to offer this world and everyone in it. Ron has touched and made such a positive impact on so many peoples lives through giving them back their health and life through his compassion, patience and healing which can only come from the heart. Not only that, but Ron has also taught many, many people how to heal themselves and others. I am one of those people, and I wouldn't be where I am today in the health and healing field, if it wasn't for Ron and the knowledge he has shared with me.

My love and sincere gratitude to you, Ron and Gloria.

Melita Curtis - Australia